The B... e

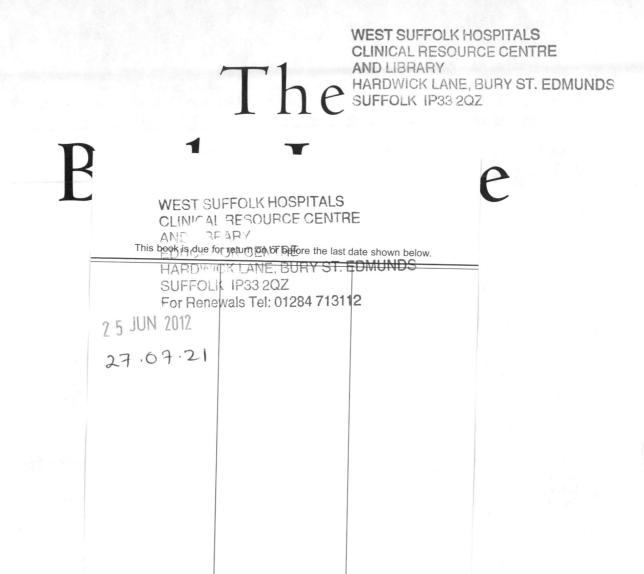

THOMAS F. CASH, PH.D.

New Harbinger Publications, Inc.

Publisher's Note

This publication is designed to provide accurate and authoritative information in regard to the subject matter covered. It is sold with the understanding that the publisher is not engaged in rendering psychological, financial, legal, or other professional services. If expert assistance or counseling is needed, the services of a competent professional should be sought.

Copyright © 2008 by Thomas F. Cash, Ph.D.
New Harbinger Publications, Inc.
5674 Shattuck Avenue
Oakland, CA 94609
www.newharbinger.com

Acquired by Tesilya Hanauer; Cover design by Amy Shoup; Edited by Kayla Sussell

Library of Congress Cataloging-in-Publication Data

Cash, Thomas F.
    The body image workbook : an eight-step program for learning to like your looks / Thomas F. Cash. -- 2nd ed.
        p. cm.
    Includes bibliographical references (p.   ).
    ISBN-13: 978-1-57224-546-4 (pbk. : alk. paper)
    ISBN-10: 1-57224-546-8 (pbk. : alk. paper) 1. Body image. 2. Body image--Problems, exercises, etc. 3. Self-acceptance. I. Title.
    BF697.5.B63C367 2008
    306.4'613--dc22

                            2008016271

FSC
Mixed Sources
Product group from well-managed
forests and other controlled sources

Cert no. SW-COC-002283
www.fsc.org
© 1996 Forest Stewardship Council

10 09 08
10 9 8 7 6 5 4 3 2 1
First printing

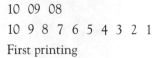

With my heartfelt appreciation,
I dedicate this work to Natalie.
She is my true love, my best friend, and my wife.
She enhances each moment of my life,
as she will "forever and four days."

Contents

STEP 6

STEP 7

STEP 8

AFTERWORD

Preface

For thirty-five years, I have devoted my career to the psychology of physical appearance. The most inspiring aspects of my work have concerned body image and how to prevent and alleviate body image problems. At the core of my professional pursuits is psychological science, which I believe informs us about how best to change lives and ameliorate human suffering.

This book builds on its earlier versions, particularly the 1997 edition, by incorporating both scientific and clinical advances from the burgeoning literature on body image development, assessment, and treatment. Indeed, in 2004 I founded a new scholarly journal, *Body Image: An International Journal of Research*, which publishes excellent and informative work on body image and human appearance. This revised edition of *The Body Image Workbook* notably integrates the new and popular disciplines of mindfulness, acceptance, and expressive writing with well established, effective cognitive and behavioral procedures for body image change. My heartfelt wish is that this book will genuinely help readers develop a more satisfying and accepting relationship with their body and will aid the therapists who may be guiding them.

My career has been blessed by opportunities to work with wonderful students, both undergraduates and graduates. Over the years, some of my doctoral students and I have conducted and published research concerning the treatment of body image difficulties and disorders. I appreciate these meaningful collaborations with Jonathan Butters, Jill Grant, Danielle Lavallee, Melissa Strachan Kinser, Joshua Hrabosky, and Kristin Grasso.

I must also acknowledge three eminent psychologists who have given me immense inspiration and valued friendship for many years. Kevin Thompson, at the University of South Florida, is undoubtedly one of the most prolific body image researchers in the world. His excellent insights and investigations have contributed greatly to my knowledge and to the field. Tom Pruzinsky, at Quinnipiac University, is the most genuinely compassionate person I know. His efforts to understand and improve the quality of life among individuals with disfiguring physical conditions are widely respected and appreciated. At the University of Pennsylvania School of Medicine, David Sarwer is a brilliant scientist whose scholarship richly informs us about body image issues in obesity, cosmetic surgery, and dermatology. I have enjoyed the privilege of collaborating with him on several projects. I am very grateful to each of you, my friends.

In the preparation of this new edition, I profited greatly from the additional editorial eyes of Natalie Cash, Jonathan Rudiger, and Erin Engle. I appreciate their diligent feedback on the accuracy and clarity of my writing.

New Harbinger is an impressively supportive publisher that truly cares about its authors, its readers, and the publication of highly reputable products that benefit therapeutic practitioners and the public. I sincerely thank Kayla Sussell, Tesilya Hanauer, Jess Beebe, and Matt McKay for skillfully assisting me in making this new edition of *The Body Image Workbook* the best that it can be.

Taking Steps to a Better Body Image

We all live embodied lives. *Body image* refers to how you personally experience your embodiment. More than a mental picture of what you look like, your body image consists of your personal relationship with your body—encompassing your perceptions, beliefs, thoughts, feelings, and actions that pertain to your physical appearance. In other words, body image is not a simple, singular thing. It is something quite complex and multifaceted. To get some idea of how complex this issue can be, ask yourself the following questions about your own body image:

- Are there aspects of your physical appearance that you really dislike?

- Do you think more about what you dislike about your looks than about what you like?

- Do you spend a lot of time worrying about what others think of your looks?

- Are your looks really important to you in determining your self-worth?

- Do the same old negative thoughts about your looks keep popping into your head and playing like a broken record?

- Do you avoid particular activities or situations because you feel physically self-conscious?

- Do you spend a lot of time, effort, or money attempting to "repair" your looks or trying to achieve physical perfection?

- Do you often rely on clothes or cosmetics to try to cover up the "flaws" in your appearance?

- Do you often search for the ultimate diet, the most effective body-shaping exercise, the right clothes, or the most flattering cosmetics or hairstyle?

- Do your feelings about your looks get in the way of accepting yourself or enjoying your everyday life?

- Do you have difficulty accepting the body that you live in? Would you rather be living somewhere else?

WHY DOES YOUR BODY IMAGE MATTER?

Your affirmative answers to these questions indicate that your body image presents some difficulties for you. You are not alone. In a large, scientific study of body image experience among college students (Williams, Cash, and Santos 2004), we discovered that 46 percent of our participants had some degree of body image discontent or difficulties. These people were evenly split into two groups. One group reported dissatisfaction with one or more aspects of their appearance, but their discontent didn't cause them considerable distress or impairment in their everyday lives. For the second group, however, their dissatisfaction was more extreme and was associated with a range of emotional and behavioral problems. Having a negative body image spawns other problems in living. Following are some of the most frequent troubles that can and do arise.

Often a poor body image lowers self-esteem. Poor self-esteem means feeling inadequate as a person; it means you have low self-worth and don't highly value yourself. As much as one-third of your self-esteem is related to how positive or negative your body image is. If you don't like your body, it's difficult to like the person who lives there—you!

Body image is integral to gender identity—your feelings of manliness or masculinity, or your feelings of womanliness or femininity. Some people believe that they don't have the physical qualities necessary to experience themselves as particularly masculine or feminine (like tallness or muscularity for guys, or thinness and having delicate features for women). This can diminish their sense of how acceptable they feel they are to others. A negative body image can cause interpersonal anxiety. If you can't accept your looks, you most likely assume others don't like your looks either. As a result, you feel self-conscious and inadequate in some of your social interactions. Fearful of social inspection and social rejection, you may even shy away from situations in which you feel that your appearance is on trial. And, of course, if nothing is ventured nothing is gained—especially fun and friendships.

If your physical self-consciousness spills into your sexually intimate relationships, it can jeopardize your capacity for sexual fulfillment. If you believe your naked body is ugly or unacceptable, sex becomes anxiety producing. Sex researchers and therapists have found that one cause of sexual difficulties is *Spectatoring*—the self-conscious scrutiny of one's own body during sex instead of immersion in the sensate experience itself. By dwelling on worries about your attractiveness or on maneuvers to hide your body from your partner's view or touch, sex becomes an act of apprehension and avoidance. If you switch off the lights to cloak your body in darkness, you may also be switching off your pleasure!

For example, in 1991, Dr. Jill Hangen and I conducted a study of body image and sexuality. We compared fifty women who were highly self-conscious about their body's appearance during sex and fifty women who weren't. Body-conscious women reported that they had orgasms in an average of only 42 percent of their lovemaking occasions—versus an average of 73 percent of the time for less physically self-conscious women. A negative body image can make it hard to give and receive sexual intimacy.

Depression and a negative body image are often intertwined. Depression can lead people to detest their looks and vice versa. Self-disparagement and thoughts of hopelessness and helplessness about what you look like are depressing. In turn, this despondency, like quicksand, can further trap you in self-criticisms of your body. It becomes a vicious cycle of despair.

As I'll discuss later in this introduction, a negative body image can bring about eating disturbances, such as anorexia nervosa or bulimia nervosa. These are problems that gradually build over time. If you worry about looking fat, you may diet and exercise to excess. Chronic dieting may lead to binge eating, which can precipitate purging. Not only does having a negative, "fat-phobic" body image predispose you to disturbed patterns of eating, but having an eating disorder undermines your body image. Changing a negative body image is as important to preventing eating disorders as it is to conquering them.

So a negative body image is bad news. Not only are you unhappy with your physical appearance, this can also diminish your quality of life. But here's the good news: A problematic, unsatisfying body image can be changed. The fact that our survey revealed that 54 percent of participants have a favorable, self-accepting body image proves that having a positive body image is really possible (Williams, Cash, and Santos 2004).

The Body Image Workbook will teach you how to transform your relationship with your body from a self-defeating struggle to an experience of body acceptance and enjoyment. Before delving into the details of this program, I want to tell you how it came to be and how it can help you.

A SCIENTIFIC APPROACH TO BODY IMAGE IMPROVEMENT

This program for body image change didn't come to me in a dream or in a rainbow vision on a rainy day. For thirty-five years I have devoted my career as a clinical and research psychologist to the psychology of physical appearance. I understand how human appearance affects human lives, especially how body image develops and influences the quality of life. Rooted in scientific psychology, this workbook reflects an active, *cognitive behavioral* approach to body image change that I began to develop in the 1980s. This approach translates knowledge from psychological science to help people change how they think, act, and feel in order to have happier, more fulfilling lives.

My doctoral students and I have carried out many scientific studies to be sure that the program really works in various formats, including a self-help format. I have continued to refine the program and have published manuals (Cash and Butters 1986), tapes (Cash 1991), and self-help books (Cash 1995c; 1997) to describe my program in detail and to facilitate its use by therapists and by the public. This extensively revised edition of *The Body Image Workbook* consists of further enhancements to make it the best that it can be.

Over the past twenty years, the effectiveness of this approach to body image improvement has been tested in clinical trials at various universities and clinics around the world. Scholarly reviews of the scientific research verify that cognitive behavioral body image therapy can produce meaningful improvements in how people feel about their physical appearance (see Hrabosky and Cash 2007; Jarry and Berardi 2004; Jarry and Ip 2005). Furthermore, these improvements enhance self-esteem, promote comfort and contentment in interpersonal and sexual relations, and reduce the risk of developing an eating disorder. Researchers have also found that a cognitive behavioral program works better than more traditional "talk therapy."

HELP YOURSELF TO WHAT YOU NEED

This revised *Body Image Workbook* represents the newest generation of the program. The workbook has been updated, reorganized, and presented in a more streamlined, user-friendly manner than the first edition. It incorporates new scientific knowledge about body image and about contemporary cognitive behavioral approaches to human change. It is for people who are dissatisfied with their looks and want to do something about it. This book is for women and men, teenagers and adults. It is for average-looking folks and for those who "look different"—whether fat or thin, tall or short, disfigured or a "perfect 10."

So, this book is for anyone with a negative body image, right? Actually, it's not. Sometimes a negative body image is part of a more complex problem. The following mental health problems require more than body image self-help: anorexia nervosa, bulimia nervosa, binge-eating disorder, and body dysmorphic disorder. Because I want you to be sure that *The Body Image Workbook* is appropriate for you, I will describe each of these four psychological difficulties.

Eating Disorders

Do you have or think you might have an eating disorder that is driven in part by your body image struggles? To overcome these three eating disorders requires professional assistance: *Anorexia nervosa* is a disorder of self-starvation in pursuit of thinness. It affects about 1 percent of adolescent girls and young women. Their fear of weight gain and their perception of themselves as fat, even when they are emaciated and physically ill, is intensely overwhelming. Controlling their weight and physical appearance seems to be the only way to control their lives. What begins as a refusal to eat becomes an inability to eat. Unfortunately, 10 to 15 percent of those with anorexia nervosa die from the condition, making it the most lethal of all mental disorders (American Psychiatric Association 2000).

Bulimia nervosa is a more widely prevalent eating disorder, occurring in an estimated 3 percent of young women (American Psychiatric Association 2000). This disorder entails recurrent eating binges; that is, the rapid consumption of large quantities of food in a very brief period. Usually carried out secretly, these binges feel out of control. After the binge comes the purge, an attempt to negate the binge and reduce the fear and the likelihood of weight gain. The purge may involve self-induced vomiting, but it may also involve the excessive, compensatory use of laxatives, diuretics, dietary fasts, or vigorous exercise. People with bulimia nervosa not only hate their body shape and weight, but their eating problem traps them in a vicious, unhealthy cycle. Their body hatred and feelings of guilt, depression, and self-loathing just keep diminishing the quality of their lives and their ability to control their eating behavior.

In a third eating disorder, binges take place without efforts to purge or to compensate for the excessive food intake. This is *binge-eating disorder*, sometimes called compulsive overeating. Understandably, binges often lead to feeling out of control, weight gain, and an even more negative body image. Binge eaters represent about 3 percent of the general population, 8 percent of obese women and men, and a greater percentage of people who seek professional weight-loss treatment (Grilo 2002).

For good health and longevity, individuals with eating disorders must gain control over their problematic eating behaviors. But they must also learn to think and feel differently about their looks so that their feelings about their weight or shape no longer define their self-worth. Without repairing their body image, they risk returning to the same old patterns of self-starvation or binges and purges. Although a negative body image is a core aspect of their problems, body image therapy isn't their sole solution.

Body Dysmorphic Disorder

For some people, perhaps up to 2 percent of the general population, an obsessive preoccupation with their appearance is the severe problem known as *body dysmorphic disorder* or *BDD*—the disorder of imagined ugliness (Phillips 2005). They have a grossly distorted view of what they look like. Others who look at them think that they either look fine or have a barely noticeable "defect." Although eating disorders are more common among females than males, BDD affects the sexes equally. Eating disorders involve body weight and shape concerns, but BDD entails other concerns, including facial features, complexion, and hair.

One subtype of BDD is called *muscle dysmorphia*, which is a preoccupation with muscularity even among those who are well built. Individuals with BDD may spend hours every day checking their "deformity" in the mirror and attempting to hide it or fix it. Social events may be avoided or self-consciously endured. Their desire to "fix their flaws" may motivate a relentless search for surgical or medical solutions. Those with muscle dysmorphia often compulsively engage in bodybuilding exercise and are at risk for the abuse of anabolic steroids and supplements to bulk up.

ADDITIONAL HELP

Can the solutions offered in this workbook help those with an extremely negative body image and an eating disorder or BDD? Yes and no. Research confirms that the use of this cognitive behavioral approach can greatly help people with these disorders, but the complexity and severity of these problems often make a purely self-help program less useful than therapist-managed treatment (Jarry and Ip 2005; Latner and Wilson 2007).

In recent years, effective treatments have emerged for eating disorders and BDD. So, if you recognize yourself in any of these descriptions, please seek professional help. Because your negative body image is an integral part of your difficulties, together you and your therapist can use this workbook to achieve maximum benefits. As a scientist and a clinical psychologist, I understand the power of professional therapy to help people make positive life changes. If you suffer from stress, anxiety, depression, relationship problems, or other difficulties that threaten your self-esteem and happiness, please get the help you need. Obtaining professional help doesn't mean that you are a weak person or a failure. It means that you wisely want your life to be better. You are entitled to seek a happy life.

The Association of Behavioral and Cognitive Therapies provides an extensive list of practitioners on its Web site at www.abct.org. Similarly, the Academy of Cognitive Therapy lists practitioners on its Web site at www.academyofct.org. Additional resources, both books and Web sites about body image, eating disorders, and BDD, are provided at the end of the book in the Recommended Resources section.

WHAT IF I WANT TO TRANSFORM MY BODY, NOT MY BODY IMAGE?

If you dislike your looks, you will understandably try to figure out how to change what you look like. Instead of thinking about an attitude adjustment, you contemplate how you can have an appearance adjustment—a slimmer physique, bigger muscles, a more youthful complexion, bigger breasts, thicker hair, or any other item on your body image wish list. Every year, millions of people diet to look thinner, exercise to look fit, purchase cosmetics to conceal flaws, or seek surgery to fix some detested feature. These remedies have one basic psychological purpose—to make the person feel better about the body she or he lives in.

What I would like you to do is this: consider the provocative possibility that your problem and its solutions have more to do with changing your body image than changing your body. Because many of you who are reading these words are either thinking about dieting or about plastic surgery, allow me to offer you my thoughts about each of these options.

Hey, Weight a Minute!

In the past thirty years, obesity rates have more than doubled in the United States and in other societies. Currently, about two-thirds of Americans are either overweight (body mass index from 25 to 25.9) or obese (BMI of 30 and higher; Hill, Catenacci, and Wyatt 2005). Rates of *bariatric surgery*, that is, surgery on the stomach and/or intestines to help a person with severe obesity lose weight, have skyrocketed in recent years. Weight concerns are a primary complaint of people with a negative body image. At any given time, about one-half of adult women and one-fourth of adult men are on a weight-loss diet. For many people, dieting is a way of life. Nevertheless, most dieters regain much of their lost weight after a year or two. Yo-yo dieters lose weight and regain it in a never-ending cycle that takes its toll on body image. In one study, for example, I discovered that after taking off an average of fifty pounds, obese dieters' body images did improve. However, after regaining an average of only five pounds a few months later, their body image gains eroded significantly (Cash 1994a).

Chronic dieting can lead to health problems, binges, emotional distress, and a possible metabolic change that increases the likelihood of weight gain. Many experts have challenged the dieting solution (see Foster and McGuckin 2002) and have written books to provide an alternative—a healthy "nondieting" lifestyle (e.g., Foreyt and Goodrick 1992; Polivy and Herman 1983).

If you are a compulsive, recurrent dieter, I know I can't readily convince you to take a different path. But I can ask that you ponder what motivates your habitual dieting. Is it a desire for health and physical well-being? Or is it a wish for attractiveness and a "fat phobia"—a fear that if you weigh more than your ideal weight you'll be a social misfit?

Effective weight management is a good idea. Rather than erratic and drastic dieting, weight control entails a healthy lifestyle that doesn't depend on the number on your bathroom scale. The sensible solution involves well-balanced nutrition, spreading out your daily food intake, and regular exercise.

It is a myth that weight loss is the only way you can accept your body if it's overweight or even just slightly heavier than you would like. For example, University of Vermont researchers (Rosen, Orosan, and Reiter 1995) provided obese people with body image therapy very similar to the program in this workbook. The program enabled participants to greatly improve how they felt about their bodies, *without* reductions in their weight.

People who need to lose weight to improve their health should separate the goals of weight loss and body acceptance. By first learning how to have a positive relationship with your imperfect body instead of a relationship full of loathing, desperation, and abuse, your ability to shed excess weight may be strengthened.

Surgical Solutions for Body Dissatisfaction

In growing numbers, men and women are seeking cosmetic surgery to change what they look like. According to the American Society of Plastic Surgeons (2007), nearly 11 million Americans received surgical or minimally invasive cosmetic procedures in 2006, at a rate 7 percent higher than in 2005, 48 percent greater than in 2000, and about 800 percent more than in 1992. The greatest recent growth is for minimally invasive procedures (chemical peels, Botox, laser treatments, microdermabrasion, and so on).

Can surgically changing your body improve your body image? In the book *Psychological Aspects of Reconstructive and Cosmetic Plastic Surgery* (Sarwer et al. 2006), my colleagues and I review the scientific evidence on this question and conclude that for many people cosmetic surgery can relieve their discontent with a specific physical characteristic. However, surgery is no magic wand; it is a catalyst for changing your relationship with yourself. I neither recommend nor oppose cosmetic surgery. Any surgery carries risks as well as potential benefits, both of which depend upon the physical and psychological makeup of the individual having the surgery, the particular surgical procedure, and the skill of the surgeon. Nonetheless, the preoccupied pursuit of surgical solutions, especially one procedure followed by another and then another, indicates there is more wrong than what one sees on the outside.

Certainly, reconstructive plastic surgery can help restore or improve the quality of life for individuals whose opportunities for human dignity, productivity, and happiness have been diminished by congenital or traumatic disfigurements. What about surgery for minor, nondisfiguring variations in appearance, such as a few sags or wrinkles or a less-than-perfect nose? Deciding to have surgery should not be like impulsively deciding to get a new hairstyle. Weighing the pros and cons requires thoughtful and knowledgeable deliberation.

My advice to you is that before you opt for extensive "exterior remodeling," work on the interior problem—your body image. After you've completed this workbook, you may no longer want to change your looks. And if you still want to change them, you'll be more likely to reap the emotional benefits from the surgery that you desire.

BUILDING A BETTER BODY IMAGE—ONE STEP AT A TIME

This workbook offers the scientific solution you've waited for—an eight-step program for enduring and gratifying changes in your body image. Let me highlight each step for you.

Step 1

First, you'll discover your body image strengths and weaknesses. You have your own distinctive appearance and your unique experience of your appearance. In this Step, you'll take scientifically developed self-tests to discover the many facets of your body image. These crucial self-discoveries will allow you to set specific goals for change.

Step 2

Why do you have a negative body image? The historical causes of a negative body image have been identified. Step 2 will fully inform you of these causes. Then, through the power of expressive writing you will come to understand how the story of your own personal body image evolved.

Step 3

Past influences are only a part of your body image. The most powerful forces come from how you think and behave in the present. In this Step, you'll learn about these forces and about mindfulness and acceptance of your here-and-now body image experiences. You will build skills to accept and neutralize your negative body image emotions. You will also begin to keep a private diary of your daily body image experiences.

Step 4

You feel what you think. How you feel about your looks is greatly influenced by your privately held beliefs, interpretations, and thought patterns. Most people have particular assumptions about the importance and influence of their looks—unchecked assumptions can lead to trouble. In this Step, you'll find out whether you unconsciously harbor ten arguable assumptions and, then, learn how to "change your mind."

Step 5

This Step involves more mind-changing. When you think about your own looks, you carry on a type of inner conversation I call *Private Body Talk*. If your Private Body Talk is permeated with mental mistakes or distortions, it will devastate your body image. In this step, you'll learn about eight common distortions. You'll listen in on your Private Body Talk, identify your own problematic thought patterns, and create a New Inner Voice to communicate with yourself about your looks and how you feel about them.

Step 6

A negative body image leads people to act in self-defeating ways to protect themselves from self-consciousness and other uncomfortable feelings. Such behaviors include *Evasive Actions*, which are habits intended to avoid these distressing experiences. These self-protective maneuvers actually make your body image even worse. In this Step, you'll learn to understand, face, and eradicate your imprisoning patterns of avoidant behavior.

Step 7

Another self-defeating behavior pattern is called *Appearance-Preoccupied Rituals*. These compulsive habits perpetuate your negative body image. This Step shows you how to rid your life of these rituals and accept your appearance as it is.

Step 8

When you reach this Step, having overcome many negative aspects of your body image, it's time to expand the genuinely positive experiences. Step 8 teaches you how to create a more confident, pleasurable, and affirming relationship with your body.

Afterword

After completing the last Step, you can take stock of your successful changes. But will they last? By being attuned to the Achilles heels of your body image and planning ahead for possible adversities, you can strengthen your new body image and ward off tough times. In this final section, you'll understand why preventative maintenance is your life insurance policy.

HOW TO MAXIMIZE YOUR BODY IMAGE BENEFITS

The Body Image Workbook isn't just for reading—it's for doing. You won't achieve the desired results from this program by being a bedtime reader, sleepily scanning a chapter or two each night until you reach the end. Each program step has the necessary self-tests to discover your personal body image difficulties and shows you how to bring about the experiences necessary for change. These experiences require that you mindfully think, plan, and act in new ways.

Each step in this workbook builds, to some degree, on the steps before it. Throughout you will find special Helpsheets that you will use while learning to accept your looks and change how you think, feel, and act in relation to your body. If you're like most people, you probably want your body image problem fixed today. Unfortunately, that's impossible. But, since each step takes only about a week or two to carry out, you'll be on your way in no time. If you'd like, first spend about an hour skimming through the entire workbook to appreciate its overall structure. Then, having reviewed the road map for your journey, venture forth—one destination at a time.

If you were my client and we were meeting face-to-face, together we would tailor this program to your specific needs. Carrying it out on your own means that you must determine how best to fit the program's steps into your daily life to suit your personal needs. The various self-tests and self-discovery assignments in the workbook will enable you to adapt the program in ways that are just right for you.

Another great idea for maximum benefits is to have one or more "body image buddies." Rather than going it alone, get an interested friend or relative to complete the program with you. Get together regularly, in person or by phone or e-mail, to discuss what you're doing and to encourage each other. If you don't have a buddy who wants to carry out the program, there may be someone else who is close to you, like a spouse, parent, best friend, or roommate, who would be willing to be your cheerleader. Enlist his or her support. This kind of support really helps to keep you motivated and on track.

So now I turn this opportunity for change over to you. And as you turn the pages, you will begin learning how to accept the body you live in.

Discovering Your Personal Body Image

Your journey toward body image change and acceptance begins with self-understanding. As conveyed by the adage "Know thyself," you must first seek specific knowledge about your own personal body image. However, because we often obtain insight about ourselves by trying to understand others, let's first consider the experiences of three people—Emily, Andrew, and Katlin—who are all having body image problems.

THREE PEOPLE WITH A NEGATIVE BODY IMAGE

Emily is a nineteen-year-old college student—bright, energetic, and sociable—whom most people would describe as nice-looking. Her weight and height are average and she has pretty blue eyes and a contagious smile. But this is not how Emily sees herself. She complains, "My big butt and fat thighs totally mess up my looks." She's preoccupied with her weight. She admits liking the color and style of her strawberry blonde hair, and she describes her upper body shape as "okay, I guess." But she has no particular feelings about most other areas of her body.

Whenever Emily goes to the gym or meets someone new (especially guys) on campus, at work, or at a social event, she's hit by a wave of self-consciousness and feels as if her body is under a microscope. Another upsetting situation occurs whenever she weighs herself and sees that she's a few pounds heavier than she'd like to be. She gets especially bothered about her body whenever she wears any snug clothing—for example, a bathing suit at the pool, or spandex workout shorts at the gym. In these situations, a familiar pattern of thoughts runs through Emily's mind: "I'm the fattest person here. I look like a blimp. I wish I could disappear. I hate feeling this way." She rarely has pleasant thoughts about her looks, unless a girlfriend compliments an outfit she's wearing. But even compliments readily lead to self-critical thoughts, such as "The outfit would look a lot better if my butt didn't stick out so much."

Because of Emily's discomfort about her looks, she sometimes avoids going to parties, especially if she knows there will be new people to meet at the event. She also avoids going to the beach or pool. When attending aerobics class, Emily sneaks into the back of the room after the class has begun. To lose weight, she's always trying out a new fad diet. Her former boyfriend thought she looked fine, but her "insane obsession with her looks" made no sense to him, and he became exasperated with her.

Andrew is a forty-year-old divorced stockbroker. He's slender, has a nicely trimmed beard, and is quite the dresser. He deplores his receding hairline and thinning hair. He's also dissatisfied with his muscularity, believing that his lack of bulging muscles makes him "look like a loser." He feels "cheated in the looks department." Once his thoughts zoom in on his appearance, as they often do, Andrew becomes irritable and despondent for the rest of the day. He's convinced that no woman will ever find him attractive enough to date. But, sometimes, if someone does seem interested in him, he wonders what's wrong with her.

Several situations predictably provoke Andrew's body image distress. When he's hanging out with guys he thinks are good-looking or who have lots of hair or well-defined muscles, Andrew compares his looks with theirs and he becomes filled with bitterness. Before going to work, he scrutinizes himself in the mirror, inspects his balding head, and examines his flexed muscles from every angle. Andrew's thoughts about his appearance are angry and self-disparaging. "I look like a damned wimp. It's totally unfair." He thinks, "I look worse every day. The more hair I lose, the dumber I look."

So how does Andrew cope? To escape feeling too "skinny," he avoids hanging out with well-built men as much as he can. From time to time he lifts weights at home (the gym is too intimidating), but he is impatient for noticeable changes so he quickly gives up working out. He wears baseball caps, even indoors, to hide his hair loss. He's tried plenty of hair-growth regimens, but they didn't work for him. Rather than asking a woman for a date and risking rejection, he goes to movies and parties alone, if at all.

Katlin is thirty-one-years-old and has been married to Patrick for ten years. They have two children and Katlin also teaches high school English. About three years ago, Katlin was involved in a near-fatal automobile accident that left her face severely lacerated and burned. Despite the improvements that she obtained from plastic surgery, her face remains visibly scarred, mostly on her chin, right cheek, and forehead. These physical changes have scarred her body image as well.

She is preoccupied with how she looks to others and what she believes they must be thinking about her. She is extremely aware of strangers' stares and is seldom willing to be in public places with her kids, fearing that they will be uncomfortable being seen with her. Sometimes when she's teaching, if she notices students whispering or giggling, she wonders if they are making fun of her looks. Before leaving the house, she always applies a thick coat of cosmetic concealer. In social situations, she tries to stand to the left of people so they cannot see the right side of her face. Patrick worries about her difficulties with "looking different" and about the fact that even though she is physically capable of smiling, she almost never smiles anymore. She fantasizes that another cosmetic surgery will make her look "normal" again. Sometimes, Katlin looks at photos of herself taken before the accident and cries. "I'll never be me again," she sobs.

SELF-DISCOVERY WITH THE BODY IMAGE SELF-TESTS

Each person's body image is as unique as a fingerprint. Emily, Andrew, and Katlin all have negative body images, but if you look more closely you'll see the experience is unique to each person. They dislike different physical features, are distressed by different triggering events, have different thoughts and emotions, and handle their problems differently. What these three people do have in common is that, like you, they are tired of struggling with their negative body images.

Now it's time to discover more about your own unique body image—both your strengths and your vulnerabilities. On the following pages, you'll find a series of self-tests that probe your personal body image experiences in detail. When you complete them, each scientifically developed test will provide you with a fine-tuned, informative summary of certain crucial facets of your body image (Cash 2008).

After you've taken all six tests, I'll show you exactly how to score them. Don't worry; you don't have to be a math genius to do this. Then, once you've computed your scores, I'll guide you in their interpretation.

THE BODY IMAGE EVALUATION TEST

On this first self-test, you will discover your *evaluative body image*. This refers to how you feel about your appearance in general as well as about particular physical characteristics or features. Put a check mark in the column that expresses how dissatisfied or satisfied you are with each characteristic listed.

Physical Characteristics	Very Dissatisfied	Mostly Dissatisfied	Mostly Satisfied	Very Satisfied
1. Overall appearance				
2. Face (facial features, complexion)				
3. Hair (color, thickness, texture)				
4. Lower torso (buttocks, hips, thighs, legs)				
5. Midtorso (waist, stomach)				
6. Upper torso (chest or breasts, shoulders, arms)				
7. Muscle tone				
8. Weight				
9. Height				
10. Any other physical characteristic that you dislike? _____				

THE BODY IMAGE THOUGHTS TEST

In the course of day-to-day life, thoughts about your appearance may run through your mind. This self-test lists some of these thoughts. Simply read each thought and decide how often, if at all, it has occurred to you in your daily life during the past month. For each thought, place a checkmark in the column that indicates how often the thought has occurred. In making this decision, don't take any listed thought too literally. Your own thoughts might be similar in content, but consist of different words. For example, you may not have the identical thought "I am unattractive," but you may have equivalent thoughts like "I'm ugly," or "I look awful."

Body Image Thoughts	Rarely or Never	Once Every Several Days	Daily or Almost Daily
1. Why can't I ever look good?			
2. My life is lousy because of how I look.			
3. My looks make me a nobody.			
4. They (other people) look better than I do.			
5. It's just not fair that I look the way I do.			
6. With my looks, nobody is ever going to love me.			
7. I wish I were better-looking.			
8. I wish I looked like someone else.			
9. They (other people) won't like me because of how I look.			
10. Something about my looks has to change.			

Body Image Thoughts	Rarely or Never	Once Every Several Days	Daily or Almost Daily
11. How I look is ruining everything for me.			
12. They (other people) are noticing what's wrong with my looks.			
13. They (other people) are thinking I'm unattractive.			
14. My clothes don't look good on me.			
15. I wish they (other people) wouldn't look at me.			
16. I can't stand my appearance anymore.			
17. They (other people) are judging me because of what I look like.			
18. There's nothing I can do to look good.			
19. I can't do that (something you're invited to or expected to do) because of my looks.			
20. I've got to look just right to do that (something you're invited to or expected to do).			

THE BODY IMAGE DISTRESS TEST

Negative body image emotions, such as anxiety, disgust, despondency, anger, frustration, envy, shame, or self-consciousness, crop up in different situations for different people. In the next self-test, you are asked to think about occasions when you've been in each of twenty situations. Place a check mark in the column to indicate how often you've had negative emotions about your appearance in each situation. Of course, there may be some listed situations that you haven't encountered or some that you avoided. If so, simply indicate how often you probably would have had distressing emotions if you had been in those situations.

Body Image Situations	Rarely or Never	Once Every Several Days	Daily or Almost Daily
1. At social gatherings where I know few people			
2. When I look at myself in the mirror			
3. When people see me before I've "fixed up"			
4. When I am with attractive people of my own sex			
5. When I am with attractive people of the opposite sex			
6. When someone looks at parts of my appearance that I dislike			
7. When I look at my nude body in the mirror			
8. When I am trying on new clothes at the store			
9. After I have eaten a full meal			
10. When I see attractive people on television or in magazines			

Body Image Situations	Rarely or Never	Once Every Several Days	Daily or Almost Daily
11. When I get on the scale to weigh myself			
12. When anticipating or having sexual relations			
13. When I'm already in a bad mood about something else			
14. When the topic of conversation pertains to physical appearance			
15. When someone comments unfavorably on my appearance			
16. When I see myself in a photograph or videotape			
17. When I think about what I wish I looked like			
18. When I think about how I may look in the future			
19. When I am with a certain person			
20. During certain recreational activities			

THE APPEARANCE IMPORTANCE TEST

People have various beliefs and experiences about the meaning and importance of their physical appearance. Some of these beliefs are reflected in the statements in this next self-test. Read each statement and decide whether it is personally mostly true or mostly false for you. Record your answers with a check mark in the appropriate column beside each statement.

Experiences and Beliefs About Your Appearance	Mostly True	Mostly False
1. When I see good-looking people, I wonder about how my own looks measure up.		
2. When something makes me feel good or bad about my looks, I tend to dwell on it.		
3. If I like how I look on a given day, it's easy to feel happy about other things.		
4. When I meet people for the first time, I wonder what they think about how I look.		
5. In my everyday life, lots of things happen that make me think about what I look like.		
6. If I dislike how I look on a given day, it's hard to feel happy about other things.		
7. I fantasize about what it would be like to be better-looking than I am.		
8. By controlling my appearance, I can control many of the social and emotional events in my life.		
9. My appearance is responsible for much of what's happened to me in my life.		
10. I often compare my appearance to that of other people I see.		

Experiences and Beliefs About Your Appearance	Mostly True	Mostly False
11. If somebody had a negative reaction to what I look like, it would bother me.		
12. My physical appearance has a big influence on my life.		

THE BODY IMAGE COPING TEST

In the course of everyday life, there are situations and events that can negatively affect our body image. These situations and events are called *body image threats or challenges*, because they threaten or challenge our ability to feel okay about how we look. Listed below are some of the ways that people may try to cope with body image threats or challenges. For each item, think about how much it characterizes how you usually cope or probably would cope with an event or situation that poses a threat or a challenge to your feelings about your body image. Indicate with a check mark whether each coping reaction is or is not characteristic of you. It doesn't matter how helpful or unhelpful your ways of coping are. Don't answer based on how you wish you reacted. Just be truthful.

Coping Reactions	Mostly Is Like Me	Mostly Is Not Like Me
1. I spend extra time trying to fix what I don't like about my looks.		
2. I think about how I could cover up what's troublesome about my looks.		
3. I do many things to try to look more attractive.		
4. I spend a lot of time in front of the mirror.		
5. I think about what I should do to change my looks.		
6. I fantasize about looking different.		
7. I seek reassurance about my looks from other people.		
8. I compare my appearance to that of physically attractive people.		
9. I make a lot of special efforts to look my best.		
10. I make a special effort to hide or cover up what's troublesome about my looks.		

Coping Reactions	Mostly Is Like Me	Mostly Is Not Like Me
11. I try to tune out my thoughts and feelings.		
12. I eat something to help me deal with the situation.		
13. I avoid looking at myself in the mirror.		
14. I tell myself that I am helpless to do anything about the situation.		
15. I withdraw and interact less with others.		
16. I make no attempt to cope or deal with the situation.		
17. I try to ignore the situation and my feelings.		
18. I react by overeating.		
19. I consciously do something that might make me feel good about myself as a person.		
20. I remind myself of my good qualities.		
21. I tell myself that I'm just being irrational about my looks.		
22. I tell myself that the situation will pass.		
23. I try to figure out why I am challenged or threatened by the situation.		

Coping Reactions	Mostly Is Like Me	Mostly Is Not Like Me
24. I tell myself that I am probably just overreacting to the situation.		
25. I remind myself that I will feel better after a while.		
26. I tell myself that there are more important things than what I look like.		
27. I tell myself that I probably look better than I think I do.		
28. I react by being especially patient with myself.		
29. I tell myself that the situation is not that important.		

THE BODY IMAGE QUALITY OF LIFE TEST

People differ in how their body image experiences affect other aspects of their lives. Body image may have positive effects, negative effects, or no effect at all. The various ways that your own body image might influence your life are listed below. For each item, place a check mark in a column to indicate how your feelings about your appearance affect that aspect of your life. Before answering each item, think carefully about the answer that is most accurate about how your body image usually affects you.

Aspects of Your Life	Mostly a Negative Effect	No Effect	Mostly a Positive Effect
1. My basic feelings about myself—feelings of personal adequacy and self-worth			
2. My feelings about my adequacy as a man or woman—feelings of masculinity or femininity			
3. My interactions with people of my own sex			
4. My interactions with people of the opposite sex			
5. My experiences when I meet new people			
6. My experiences at work or at school			
7. My relationships with friends			
8. My relationships with family members			
9. My day-to-day emotions			
10. My satisfaction with my life in general			

Aspects of Your Life	Mostly a Negative Effect	No Effect	Mostly a Positive Effect
11. My feelings of acceptability as a sexual partner			
12. My enjoyment of my sex life			
13. My ability to control what and how much I eat			
14. My ability to control my weight			
15. My activities for physical exercise			
16. My willingness to do things that might call attention to my appearance			
17. My daily grooming activities (i.e., getting dressed and physically ready for the day)			
18. How confident I feel in my everyday life			
19. How happy I feel in my everyday life			

SCORING YOUR BODY IMAGE SELF-TESTS

After taking the tests, most people say that it was an eye-opening experience. They become more self-aware and have a somewhat greater realization of how their body image influences their emotions and their lives. Of course, putting these experiences under a microscope may be a bit bothersome. So, if you want to take a breather before scoring your tests, feel free to do so. Your discomfort will pass and you'll be ready to pick up where you left off.

Let's score your self-tests one at a time. Follow my instructions below for each test. Enter each score you obtain in the Body Image Profile below.

The Body Image Evaluation Test

Here you have indicated the areas or aspects of your appearance that you like or dislike. Count the number of characteristics with which you are Very Dissatisfied (in column 1) and multiply it times 2. Count the number you rated Mostly Dissatisfied (i.e., your check mark is in column 2). Add these two sums to obtain your Body Image Evaluation score. Enter this score (from 0 to 20) in your Body Image Profile below.

The Body Image Thoughts Test

On this test you revealed how often, over the past month, you've had various negative thoughts about your looks. To compute your score, first count the number of check marks you placed in the middle column (Once Every Several Days). Next count the thoughts occurring Daily or Almost Daily (check marks in the last column) and multiply this second number times 2. Add the two sums and enter your Body Image Thoughts score (0 to 40) in your Body Image Profile below.

The Body Image Distress Test

This test focuses on situations and events that lead to body image discomfort or distress. First, add up the check marks you put in the middle column (Sometimes). Next, add up the check marks in the last column (Often) and multiply that number by 2. The sum of these two values is your Body Image Distress score (ranging from 0 to 40) to enter on your Body Image Profile.

The Appearance Importance Test

This test is easy to score. Count how many statements that you marked as Mostly True for you and enter this Appearance Importance score (from 0 to 12) in your Body Image Profile.

The Body Image Coping Test

This test has three scores that reflect different coping strategies that people use to handle body image threats and challenges. The first coping strategy is called Appearance Fixing and its score is the number of check marks you entered in the first column (Mostly Is Like Me) for items 1 through 10. The second score is for coping by Experiential Avoidance—and that is the number of Mostly Is Like Me check marks for items 11 through 18. Finally, count the Mostly Is Like Me check marks for items 19 through 29 to get your score for coping by Positive Rational Acceptance. Enter each score in your Body Image Profile.

The possible range of scores is 0 to 10 for Appearance Fixing, 0 to 8 for Experiential Avoidance, and 0 to 11 for Positive Rational Acceptance.

The Body Image Quality of Life Test

Your final test enables you to understand how your body image affects you and your life. You need to calculate two scores. The first one is the Negative Impact score, which is the number of times (from 0 to 19) you checked Mostly a Negative Effect, in the first column. The second score, Positive Impact, is the number of check marks (from 0 to 19) in the last, Mostly a Positive Effect, column. Enter these two different scores in your Body Image Profile.

SELF-DISCOVERY HELPSHEET: YOUR BODY IMAGE PROFILE

Body Image Test Scores	Body Image Zones		
	Acceptance Zone	Risky Zone	Problem Zone
Body Image Evaluation ____ + ____ = ____	0 I	2 3 4 5	6-10 11-15 16-20
Body Image Thoughts ____ + ____ = ____	0-1 2-3 4-5	6-8 9-11 12-14 15-17	18-22 3-29 30-40
Body Image Distress ____ + ____ = ____	0-1 2-3 4-5	6-8 9-11 12-14 15-17	18-22 23-29 30-40
Appearance Importance ____	0 I 2	3 4 5 6	7-8 9-10 11-12
Body Image Coping Appearance Fixing ____ Experiential Avoidance ____ Positive Rational Acceptance ____	0 I 2 0 I II 10 9 8 7	3 4 5 6 2 3 4 5 6 5 4 3	7 8 9 10 6 7 8 2 I 0
Body Image Quality of Life Negative Impact ____ Positive Impact ____	0 I 19 18	2-3 4-5 6-7 16-17 14-15 12-13	8-11 12-15 16-19 8-11 4-7 0-3

INTERPRETATION OF YOUR BODY IMAGE TESTS

You have taken the comprehensive self-tests of body image and, in the process, have already begun to realize some key things about your own body image. Now let's take your self-discovery to the next level and learn what your test scores really mean. I will guide you in interpreting your test results so that you can determine exactly what you need to change.

Three Body Image Zones

On the right side of the Body Image Profile under Body Image Zones, for each score please circle the value or range that represents your score. This will place each test score on a continuum that will help you understand the meaning of the score in terms of three Body Image Zones—the Acceptance Zone, the Risky Zone, and the Problem Zone.

Scores in the *Acceptance Zone* reflect a positive, healthy aspect of your body image. There's not much that needs improvement on this facet. Individuals with the best body image will have lots of scores in this zone. The main purpose of this workbook is to help you have more scores in the Acceptance Zone.

Scores in the *Risky Zone* signal a warning and identify directions for change that this workbook will make possible. Those facets of your body image in this zone cause hassles or difficulties for you sometimes and in some situations. The closer a score is to the Acceptance Zone the better; and the closer it is to the Problem Zone, the more body image difficulties you have. Risky Zone scores pinpoint aspects of your body image with definite room for improvement that you will want to work on.

Scores in or near the *Problem Zone* wave red flags. These aspects of your body image are especially troublesome for you and make important contributions to a negative body image. Problem Zone scores highlight key areas to target in your efforts to change and become more accepting of your physical appearance.

Now let's examine each of your test results in detail to understand what your scores can tell you about your body image. You should realize, however, that scores are only numbers and cannot be perfectly precise for specific people. These test results are tools for self-discovery, not pronouncements of absolute truth. I will offer interpretations as food for thought. Ultimately, the most important insights must come from you. So, take the time you may need to really ponder what I suggest. Does it fit? When discussing your test results, I will ask you as much as I tell you.

Body Image Evaluation: Where Does It Hurt?

People with Risky Zone and Problem Zone scores on this test are dissatisfied with many of their physical characteristics (Cash 2000b). Because you are probably reading this book to overcome a negative body image, don't be surprised if you score in one of these zones. There are at least two possible reasons for such scores. First, you may have several distinct sources for your displeasure. Being overly critical of your looks, you find a number of different physical attributes that you cannot accept as they are. When you look at your body, you look for trouble and are unwilling to find anything that is really

29

okay. Your body is a moving target for your discontent. Second, there's the spillover factor. Not liking your weight, for example, may spill over to any body area (e.g., lower torso, midtorso, muscle tone) that you think betrays your weight. You actually have only one complaint, but it affects your evaluation of several features.

Some people may have a low dissatisfaction score on Body Image Evaluation that is more of a problem than the low score actually implies. Often this is occurs because you are content with most of your physical characteristics except for one or two, but feel that the areas of discontent ruin your overall appearance. Did you answer that you were dissatisfied with your overall appearance on item 1? If so, are you blaming your entire body for one or two disappointing features? That can create lots of troublesome problems.

Whatever your score and whatever imperfections you focus on, eliminating any dissatisfaction is worth the effort. This workbook will help you accept your physical appearance—imperfections and all.

How Thought-Provoking Is Your Body Image?

When you took the Body Image Thoughts Test, you began to read your own mind. The test samples negative thoughts that people may have about their looks (Cash, Lewis, and Keeton 1987). Scores in the Problem Zone mean that you tend to think the worst about your looks and you think it often. You've probably convinced yourself that these mental self-criticisms are really true. As you mull over aspects of your appearance, you focus on your "flaws." You ruminate over what other people think about your looks and probably assume they judge you as disapprovingly as you do yourself. Once caught up in the stream of these thoughts, it's hard for you to ignore them. If you score in the Risky Zone, you may be milder in your self-critical thoughts, or you may put down your body in a more focused fashion, picking on some single feature. Either way, you are needling yourself—needlessly.

Let's consider the other side of the coin. How often do you have positive, self-affirming thoughts about your physical appearance? How open is your mind to pleasant, approving thoughts about your body? If you have a negative reply to these questions, why is that? Why would you close your mind to self-acceptance? Maybe you're oblivious to your physical assets, so you don't believe there's anything good to think about. Or maybe you push aside any complimentary thoughts with a "Yes but ..." followed by some self-criticism. For example, "I look pretty nice with this hairstyle, but I'm still fat."

Another reason for a deficit of self-affirming thoughts could be that you've come to believe that only vain, egotistical people think favorably of their looks. If so, then any mental compliment about your appearance may lead to a brief guilt trip, so you dismiss the positive thought with "I shouldn't be thinking that." Later in this workbook, you'll learn to give yourself permission to acknowledge and enjoy your best features—without the guilt. How would it feel if you didn't have self-critical body image thoughts running through your mind? How would it feel to have frequent self-accepting body image thoughts?

Where Are Your Body Image Land Mines?

Now let's learn more about the situations and events that trigger your troubles. Your Body Image Distress score reflects how many situations trigger you to becoming bothered or upset about your looks

(Cash 1994b; 2002b). You might feel anxiety, disgust, despondency, anger, frustration, envy, shame, or self-consciousness. If you have a score in the Problem Zone, daily life is probably like crossing a minefield, with the potential for negative emotions and experiences to erupt almost everywhere.

Scores that are in the Risky Zone indicate that you have some times and places that intensify your body image displeasure. Even if your distress is triggered by limited circumstances, you don't need the grief and can learn to eliminate it. In this workbook, you'll focus on your most provocative situations—the ones in which you're conditioned to react emotionally—and you will learn to handle these situations differently. You will learn that the situation itself doesn't cause your distress. Rather, the real culprit that upsets you is how you think about and behave in the situation.

Importance of Your Appearance: How Much Do You Bank on Your Looks?

The Appearance Importance Test taps a very important aspect of your body image (Cash and Labarge 1996; Cash, Melnyk, and Hrabosky 2004). It provides you with a measurable index to determine how much you are invested in your physical appearance for defining your identity and determining your self-worth. The more you invest, the more vulnerable you are to body image troubles and problems in your life. If you score in the Risky Zone, you believe that your appearance is moderately influential on how you think about yourself or how you believe other people think and feel about you. Scores in the Problem Zone reveal that you place excessive emphasis on your physical appearance in terms of how you think about yourself in your everyday life.

The scientific truth is that the more invested people are in their appearance, the more it preoccupies them—in their thoughts, emotions, and behaviors. If you are devoting lots of your hopes, energies, and efforts to being physically attractive or looking different than you do, especially because you believe that this is essential to your self-worth, you actually will feel little self-worth. Do yourself a favor and reread this paragraph and really think about it. Can you see how it applies to you?

Several steps in this workbook will focus on helping you to gradually deemphasize your looks and put them in a proper, happier perspective. Your looks are not everything, and you are certainly much more than your looks.

How Do You Cope with Feeling "Ugly"?

There are three basic ways that people try to handle or cope with threats or challenges to their body image (Cash, Santos, and Williams 2005). The Body Image Coping Test provides your scores for each approach—Appearance Fixing, Experiential Avoidance, and Positive Rational Acceptance. Let's try to understand each coping strategy and what your scores mean.

Appearance Fixing is a common coping strategy that involves mental and behavioral attempts to change something about your looks. When troubled by some offending physical characteristic, you may reflexively try to do something to your appearance to feel more comfortable. You might fuss and fret over the characteristic and try to cover it up to make it look better. For example, if something happens that makes you feel fat, you might put on loose-fitting clothing, start planning your next diet, or begin working out to your exercise video.

Another Appearance Fixing tactic is called *compensation*. You try to improve something specific about your looks, such as by getting a new hairstyle or buying new cosmetics or an outfit, so that you make yourself "look better in order to feel better." One additional strategy involves seeking reassurance about your looks from other people. When you ask a friend, "Do you think I look fat in this sweater?" you hope to hear "No, of course not" and have your concern fixed. You can also "fix by fantasy"— imagining how you will look after weight loss or cosmetic surgery. Later, in Step 6 of the workbook, you'll see how coping by Appearance Fixing can become a problematic pattern called Appearance-Preoccupied Rituals. You will learn how to overcome this problem.

Dealing with body image discomfort by Experiential Avoidance entails efforts to shut out or evade negative body image emotions. So you may say to yourself, "Don't think about this" or "I can't think about this." Perhaps you avoid by distracting yourself from your upsetting experience—you may watch television or eat to take your mind off of it. Often, some people cope with anticipated body image discomfort by completely avoiding the situation that they expect will elicit it. If you expect to feel self-conscious at the beach party or aerobics class, you just refuse to go. Avoidance may provide you with temporary relief, but it perpetuates your body image difficulties. In Step 3, you will begin to learn how to accept your feelings instead of avoiding them. In Step 6, you will also learn to stop playing out your Evasive Actions.

Unlike the first two strategies for managing negative body image emotions, Positive Rational Acceptance is a healthy approach. As you will see in Step 3, discomfort is neither dangerous nor revealing of some awful inner truth about you. It is merely a feeling. You can learn how to be aware of and accept that feeling, rather than trying to deny it, avoid it, transform it, or allow it to dictate what you do. In Steps 3, 4, and 5 of the workbook, you will learn from your feelings and develop a more honest, self-affirming perspective on your body image experiences.

How Does Your Body Image Influence Your Life?

As discussed in the introduction, being dissatisfied with something about your physical appearance may be no problem at all or it may be a very big problem. The difference is determined by the impact or consequences of your body image in your everyday life (Cash and Fleming 2002b; Cash, Jakatdar, and Williams 2004). Does your body image influence your feelings about yourself, your social interactions, your eating and exercise behaviors, your sexuality, and so on? It is essential for you to understand how your body image experiences affect the quality of your life. This is measured by your two Body Image Quality of Life scores. A high Negative Impact score means that your body image produces numerous disruptive, interfering effects on your life. A low Positive Impact score indicates that your view of your looks seldom gives rise to experiences of pleasure, contentment, joy, or pride. The ultimate goal of the program found in this workbook is to enhance the quality of your life by helping you improve your body image acceptance.

TRANSLATING YOUR SELF-DISCOVERIES INTO GOALS FOR CHANGE

At this point, having taken and interpreted all the self-tests, your body image should be coming into sharper focus. You should now see patterns, both your strengths and your vulnerabilities, that were not apparent to you before. You may be tempted to chastise yourself—"I can't believe my body image is so bad. I'm such a total mess!"—but I urge you to take a different, more self-accepting viewpoint. Your self-discoveries give you insights into exactly what you need to change. And this insightful knowledge is power. You could not change without it.

What Do You Need?

Let's translate your self-discoveries into specific directions for improvement. Take a look at the Needs for Change Helpsheet that follows this section. Identify and write down two or three important needs for change based on your results from each body image self-test. The Helpsheet is organized into specific topics so that you can easily translate your self-discoveries into individualized goals for change. If you go back and look at your answers to specific items on each test, you will see some of these directions for change. You may also have ideas about what you need to change that are not based on your test results.

Don't second-guess something that you need to work on by deciding that you cannot change it. Suspend judgment about what you can or cannot accomplish. Just write down the changes that you suspect or know would make your body image (and life) better. Each section of the Helpsheet has room for three needs for change. If you want to list more, use the margins or your own notebook.

Do you remember Emily, whom you met at the beginning of this chapter? Here are a few examples from her Needs for Change Helpsheet:

- "I need to stop loathing my lower body."

- "I need fewer self-critical thoughts about my weight."

- "I need to allow myself to have positive thoughts about what I like about my looks."

- "I need to become more comfortable with my looks at social events (e.g., at the pool)."

- "I need to be able to look in the mirror and not get upset."

- "I need to spend less time trying to decide what to wear before going out."

- "I need to quit comparing myself to every good-looking woman I see (especially in those in the beauty mags)."

- "I need to eat healthy instead of doing dumb diets."

- "I need to quit jockeying for the back row in aerobics class."

Here are excerpts from Andrew's needs list:

- "I need to stop being so angry at myself for my hair loss."

- "I need to quit hiding under my baseball cap, though it scares me to think about that."

- "I need to accept the fact that I'm not a muscle man and the reality is that I never will be."

- "I need to spend less time criticizing myself when I'm looking in the mirror."

- "I need to give myself credit for the fact that I work out regularly and that I'm in good shape."

- "I need to stop thinking that women consider me boring because of my looks."

- "I need to appreciate that I have nice skin, an attractive beard, and I really dress well."

- "I need to be friendlier to muscular guys. It's not their fault they're built differently than I am."

- "I need to socialize more and stop using my looks as an excuse for staying home."

- "I need to recognize that all single women aren't going to reject me for my looks and that the ones who do aren't women I ultimately want to be with anyway."

What are some of the things Katlin says she needs to change? Here they are:

- "As hard as it is to do, I need to accept that I look different now. I need to work on that."

- "I need to stop looking at my old photos, because that always upsets me."

- "I need to quit trying to make my scars invisible, because they aren't and never will be."

- "I really, really need to get more comfortable with other people looking at me."

- "I need to smile more, because everybody is more attractive when they smile."

- "I need to figure out what to say to people who seem bothered my scars."

- "I need to quit thinking that my husband and kids are ashamed of me, because I know that I'm a terrific wife and mom and that they really love me."

- "I need to realize that my appearance doesn't have to prevent my having fun, unless I let that happen."

Helpsheet for Change: My Needs for Change

Physical characteristics I need to accept more:

I need to _____

I need to _____

I need to _____

Negative body image thoughts that I most need to reduce or eliminate:

I need to _____

I need to _____

I need to _____

Situations I really need to feel more comfortable with:

I need to _____

I need to _____

I need to _____

Beliefs and behaviors I need to change to be less invested in my appearance for my self-worth:

I need to _____

I need to _____

I need to _____

Ways that I cope with my body image difficulties that I need to change:

I need to _____

I need to _____

I need to _____

The consequences (effects) of my body image difficulties I especially want (need) to change:

I need to _____

I need to _____

I need to _____

FINAL WORDS OF ENCOURAGEMENT

Each of the following chapters of *The Body Image Workbook* is chock-full of opportunities to discover additional assets and liabilities affecting your body image. And always, after you learn what's wrong, you'll then learn how to make it better.

This detailed discovery of what's risky or problematic with your body image can leave you feeling as though you're at the bottom of a mountain that you'll never be able to climb. I understand. This is a natural human feeling. A journey is often hardest at its start. Realize that the climb isn't as steep or as treacherous as it may seem at the moment. Others have taken the same path you are about to take, and they have succeeded. You've pinpointed your difficulties and used them to identify positive directions, and you can accomplish your goals one step at a time. I commend you for completing this first important step. Onward!

Understanding the Origins of Your Body Image Story

Melissa will turn thirty on her next birthday. She's struggled with her body image for as long as she can recall. When she looks at her baby pictures, all she can say is "Well, at least I was cute for a few months." What she remembers from her preschool years is a family get-together where her aunt announced loudly to everybody that Melissa looked just like Miss Piggy. Melissa can still hear all the laughter, especially her mom's and dad's. She ran to her room and cried inconsolably. Her big brother started calling her Miss Piggy, and continued doing so for years.

During elementary and middle school, Melissa had lots of friends and enjoyed sleepovers and after-school soccer games. She liked feeling athletic and being one of the best on the team. When she was ten, her coach told her she'd be a better player if she lost some weight. She decided she would, so she started discarding the lunch her mom packed for her each day. Although she never told her mother about this, Melissa figured she would understand, because her mom was always complaining about her own weight and was always on one diet or another. Melissa also recalls that her parents never told her she was pretty.

Melissa's puberty arrived at the age of twelve. This came along with a very unwelcome growth spurt. Some of the boys at school teased her about having "big boobies," and she began to feel very self-conscious about the changes her body was going through. She hated her fuller hips and dreaded having her period each month. She started wearing baggy clothing to conceal her body shape whenever possible. She quit her sports activities and focused on her straight-A academic subjects.

In high school, Melissa continued to worry about how she looked. Occasional outbreaks of acne on her face and back worsened her body image concerns. She regularly dated a guy who told her that she was beautiful. She liked that he said this but suspected it was just a ploy for having sex with her. When she did have sex with him, she insisted on having the lights off. When they broke up, she noticed that his new girlfriend was thinner than she was. She went on a diet again.

College brought Melissa continued academic success, some good female friends, and several short-term romantic relationships. She dieted often and went to the gym regularly for aerobic exercise. She also fell in love with Craig, her future husband. She describes this as the best time of her life. In her words, "I had lots of fun, discovered my love for computer science, met Craig, and lost fifteen pounds."

Landing a great job and getting married after graduation, Melissa was excited about her new life. Still, she often felt self-conscious about her body. She frequently compared herself to other women and concluded that she was either fat or unattractive. Little things about her looks bugged her, even though she knew "rationally" that she looked okay and "this shouldn't matter so much." Craig's compliments and assurances didn't help. Every morning, she weighed herself nervously. She spent lots of money shopping for new, flattering outfits. To prepare for work or a social event, she labored for more than an hour with her hair, makeup, and clothes.

Now, Melissa is tired of struggling with her body image and hates how it affects her and her life. She is beginning to see how the story of her body image unfolded from her childhood to the present. She wants to change and accept herself as she is.

THE DEVELOPMENT OF A NEGATIVE BODY IMAGE: VOICES FROM THE PAST

As you can see from Melissa's story, people don't just wake up one day with the conviction that they cannot stand their looks. Usually, they've felt this way for quite some time. Body image forms gradually, beginning in childhood. Life experiences lead some people to relate to their bodies in positive and satisfying ways, while other people travel a less enjoyable path. The factors that influence body image development can be divided into two basic categories:

1. The historical influences from your past are the forces that shaped how you came to view your appearance in the ways that you do.

2. The current influences are the events and experiences in everyday life that determine how you think, feel, and react to your looks.

You must explore each of these two influences in greater detail so that you can really understand your personal body image development. In Step 2, we focus on the historical causes. Step 3 will deal with the forces responsible for your day-to-day body image experiences.

Your basic sense of identity is rooted in your experience of being embodied. The body is the boundary between you and everything that is not you. By the age of two years, most children have self-awareness and can recognize their physical self as a reflection in the mirror. More and more, their bodily being comes to represent who they are in their own eyes. Then they begin to reflect upon how other people view their appearance.

Take a close look at figure 2.1. It identifies four categories of historical factors that govern body image development: cultural forces, interpersonal experiences, physical characteristics and changes, and individual personality traits. These factors shape all of our body image attitudes—the perceptions, beliefs, thoughts, and feelings we come to have about our physical appearance. These attitudes include not only how satisfied or dissatisfied we are with our looks, they also involve how invested we are in our physical appearance for defining who we are and who we want to be. Some events and experiences have a negative influence and others a positive influence on our unfolding body image attitudes.

To understand body image development (including your own), let's consider some of the interesting ideas and research evidence offered by psychological scientists who have studied body image (Cash and Pruzinsky 2002; Grogan 2007; Thompson 2004; Wertheim, Paxton, and Blaney 2004).

Figure 2.1
Body Image Development: Historical Influences

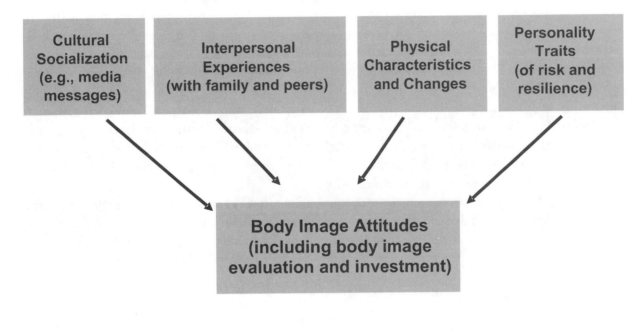

CULTURAL REFLECTIONS

By the time children attend preschool they have already started learning how society views various physical characteristics. Little kids know that lovely Cinderella wins the handsome prince; her ugly and mean stepsisters lose out. They know that Barbie and Ken have the good life, with bodies to match. They know that male superheroes and action figures have bulging muscles. Body image takes shape as children absorb concepts of what society values as attractive—how they should look. Kids also form images of what is not attractive—how they should not look. In animated cartoons and feature films for kids, the "losers" and "bad guys" are often depicted as ugly or fat. Most importantly, children begin to judge their own bodily appearance—how well does it live up to the "shoulds"? The answer can affect their sense of self-worth.

From the word go, society dictates social values and the meanings of physical appearance. Let's take a closer look at the biased lessons our culture teaches us.

My Fair Lady

The adulation of thinness hasn't occurred in some cultures to the extent that it has in Western society. For example, in societies where food is scarce and Western media are absent, a heavier body is still viewed as evidence of successful survival. In earlier times, a full-figured physique was the epitome of feminine beauty. The rounded hips and thighs of prehistoric goddesses symbolized feminine fertility. In much of the art of the fifteenth to eighteenth centuries, full-figured women were the standard of beauty. In the ancient Orient, a fat wife was such a symbol of honor for her husband that some men force-fed their wives to enhance their own social standing.

In the twentieth and twenty-first centuries, however, a thinner and less curvaceous body type has increasingly been promoted as the standard of feminine attractiveness. In the last thirty years, fashion models, film stars, and beauty pageant contestants have all become thinner, even as the majority of the female population has become heavier. As rates of anorexia nervosa and bulimia nervosa have steadily increased, emaciated "waif" models appear on magazine covers and fashion runways, in television ads, and in music videos. The message broadcast is that "thin is in and feminine." Each year *People* magazine publishes its "Most Beautiful People" list. Esthetic accolades have been given to such obviously slender bodies as those of Jessica Alba, Halle Berry, Penelope Cruz, Angelina Jolie, Alicia Keys, Nicole Kidman, Julia Roberts, and Eva Longoria—to name just a few. And as reflected by the prevalence of breast augmentation surgery—there were over 329,000 surgeries in the United States in 2006 (American Society of Plastic Surgeons 2007)—large, shapely breasts have become more important to the cultural ideal (just as they were in the middle of the twentieth century).

For the sake of beauty, women in our society are told to shave or wax their legs, armpits, and bikini areas, pluck their eyebrows, dye and either curl or straighten their hair, pierce their ears, paint their faces and all twenty nails, and walk around in uncomfortable (and sometimes dangerous) high heels. Women are also told that they should worry about unsightly age spots, split ends, the sprouting of a single gray hair, a chipped nail, and a visible panty line. It's no wonder that many girls and women feel objectified and find so many things faulty about their looks!

The Handsome Prince

Although less demanding than women's appearance standards, societal norms and expectations definitely exist for men. Guys are supposed to be tall and have broad shoulders, a muscular chest and biceps, a small rear, strong facial features, and a full head of hair. Most manly heroes and leading men are handsome hunks—George Clooney, Brad Pitt, Patrick Dempsey, Colin Farrell, Jude Law, Denzel Washington, Orlando Bloom, Richard Gere, and so on. A generation ago, John "Duke" Wayne protected his masculine "stand tall" image by refusing to appear "topless" in public—that is, without his hairpiece.

These masculine body prescriptions lead some boys and men to jeopardize their health with steroid abuse and excessive exercise. A fascinating book entitled *The Adonis Complex: The Secret Crisis of Male Body Obsession* (Pope, Phillips, and Olivardia 2000) details the difficulties of males with muscle dysmorphia, that is, those who seek a perfect muscular physique but often feel inadequate and scrawny. Today, more than ever before, men seek cosmetic surgery, including nose reshaping, liposuction, hair transplants, and face lifts. In America in 2006, they received over 250,000 surgical and 850,000 nonsurgical cosmetic procedures (American Society of Plastic Surgeons 2007). So, clearly, many men feel pressured to be physically attractive, believing that good looks are a prerequisite for success in relationships and life in general. The popular new term "metrosexual" was coined to characterize the single, heterosexual, urban male who is highly invested in his appearance and its expression of "esthetic style."

Cultures are not uniform. Every culture consists of subcultures that may differ greatly from one another. For example, within the United States, African-Americans have norms and values that do not mirror the majority culture's norms and values. With respect to physical appearance, the appreciation of a fuller-figured female body and the valuing of personal style and "attitude" in dress protect some African-American women from developing as self-deprecating a body image as European-American women (Roberts et al. 2006).

Another subculture pertains to sexual orientation. A recent scientific review (Morrison, Morrison, and Sager 2004) of studies comparing gay and lesbian people with those who are heterosexual concluded that, on average, gay men report more body dissatisfaction than heterosexual guys, perhaps in part because of excessive emphasis on appearance among gays. Research findings are less clear for lesbians, but on average they may be slightly more body accepting than heterosexual women of comparable body weight.

From Cultural Images to Body Images

In various cultures at various times, attractiveness has required decorative scars on the face, a shaved head, tattoos fully covering the body, jewels placed in holes drilled in the teeth, large disks inserted in the lips, stacked rings to elongate the neck, and the maiming of women's feet to make them petite. All these things were done, and most still are, in service of societal standards of attractiveness. Moreover, societal norms are ever-changing. For example, only a decade or so ago in Western culture, body piercing and tattooing were only popular among men—especially bikers, gangs, and prisoners. Today, body art is very popular among young women. What was once taboo has become socially acceptable and "cool."

Just as you may dismiss other cultures' foreign appearance standards as "really crazy," I urge you to begin to question the mandates of your own culture or subculture. Who are the appearance masters that you feel obliged to serve? Throughout this workbook, I'll help you defend yourself against these unhealthy messages. Right now, I want you to contemplate two crucial facts:

- **Fact 1: Societal standards can't harm you unless you buy into them.** You don't have to adopt these ideals and pressure yourself to live up to them. You don't have to allow your sense of self-worth to be determined by voices not of your choosing. If you think you should possess some trait that you believe you lack, you'll experience distress in situations that remind you of this "inadequacy."

- **Fact 2: Other people don't judge you as harshly as you judge yourself.** In numerous studies, researchers have discovered that many people demand more physical "perfection" of themselves than they think others expect of them, and even more than those others truly expect. Often, such people are out of touch with reality. Many men are often more appreciative of a heavier female body type than women believe they are. Guys don't idealize blonde beauty to the degree women assume. Likewise, lots of women don't idolize the narrowly defined images of "macho" attractiveness that men often assume they do.

INTERPERSONAL INFLUENCES

Dr. Kevin Thompson, an esteemed body image researcher at the University of South Florida, points to three pivotal sources of influence in body image development. One of these, as we've already touched upon, is the influence of our culture's mass media. The other two causes are embedded in our relationships with others—our peers and our family.

Sticks and Stones: "Hey Fatso!"

Your family has most likely taught you a lot about your own body. Parents remind you to brush your hair, put on clean clothes with patterns and colors that don't clash, and stay trim. When you were growing up, how many times did you hear "You're not really going to leave the house looking like that, are you?" Families also communicate expectations by what psychologists call *modeling*. For example, if you grow up with a parent who consistently complains about his or her appearance, you learn that looks can be something to worry about. If you have a brother or sister doted on for being attractive, you may come to feel shortchanged by your own looks. You may feel resentful and envious that you aren't as nice-looking.

Being repeatedly criticized, taunted, or teased about your appearance during the childhood or teen years can leave a lasting effect on body image development. Many adults who dislike their appearance can recall experiences of being teased or criticized as children because of their looks. Deeply etched in their memories are episodes of rebuke or ridicule for being too chubby or too skinny, too tall or too short, for having a large nose or big ears, or for how they dressed or wore their hair.

In one study (Rieves and Cash 1996), 72 percent of college students revealed that, while growing up, they had been repeatedly teased or criticized for an average of over six years, usually about their facial features or weight. Many reported having had an unwelcome nickname—Bubble Butt, Pinocchio, Freckles, Pizza Face, Four-Eyes, Carrot Top, Beanpole, or Horse Face, for example. Of those who had been teased, 71 percent said it had been moderately to very upsetting, whereas the remainder—only 29 percent—were able to shrug it off. The most common teasers were brothers and peers in general. An earlier study (Cash 1995a) revealed that 65 percent said that appearance teasing had marred their body image. Both studies revealed that a reported history of such treatment was linked to a more negative adult body image.

Teasing is just one type of appearance-related maltreatment. People who are overweight also experience other stigmatizing difficulties—for example, social exclusion, public stares, fat jokes, and shopping for clothes that fit. As a 2004 study by Annis, Cash, and Hrabosky revealed, among overweight women, experiencing such stigma during childhood, adolescence, and adulthood is subsequently associated with more body dissatisfaction, excessive psychological investment in one's appearance, and more psychological problems. Being body-stigmatized represents a contradictory, double message that one's looks are unacceptable yet essential to social and personal well-being.

As we grow and interact with our peers, the topic of physical appearance comes up fairly often, especially for females. Girls and young women engage in familiar "fat chat" with one another. They discuss weight and dieting, and the social expectation is that one is supposed to complain about being too fat. Unfortunately, this "ritual" of self-criticism seems to encourage and produce body dissatisfaction (Nichter 2000; Tucker et al. 2007). By the same token, it's difficult to imagine that "skinny talk" about male bodies would be very healthy for boys.

Romantic relationships can exert strong influences on our thoughts and feelings about our looks. Their power results from the fact that we may see an intimate partner's view of us as a valid reflection of our worth—after all, our partner "really knows us." Moreover, in a sexual relationship, the partner can see the "naked truth" of what we look like. Having a relationship in which our loved one is complimentary and accepting can promote a positive body image. Of course, the opposite is true as well. Having a partner criticize or seem oblivious to our looks can erode our body image acceptance.

You can clearly see that, as we grow up, our relationships with peers and family members can have both positive and negative effects on our body image development. In a survey of nearly five hundred college students (Cash, Rudiger, and Williams 2008), we asked them how happy they were with their appearance during childhood and during their teen years. For those who had a positive body image as children, we simply asked them to list all the factors that contributed to their acceptance of their physical appearance. You might think they would have talked about having a nice body or cute face, but less than 18 percent of their responses mentioned physical attributes as the most important influence. In both childhood and adolescence, *social support* was most often given as the primary influence, as 32 percent pointed to having good friends and family who accepted and cared about them. Moreover, our results indicated that family support was more important than peer support in childhood, while the opposite was true for adolescence.

PHYSICAL CHARACTERISTICS AND CHANGES

The human body changes dramatically at puberty. This time can also bring intense preoccupation with these changes and with physical appearance in general. Having the "right" body type, clothes, or hairstyle often becomes far more important than algebra or geography. The relative timing of physical maturation can also be important in body image development. Girls whose hips and breasts develop earlier than those of their classmates may feel self-conscious. They don't appreciate their new shape as a sign of approaching womanhood but can only see it as grotesque fat. Boys whose spurt in height and muscularity is slower than that of their peers may worry privately that their body will never catch up.

The teen years are an especially tough time for body image. Teenagers' feelings of social adequacy depend in part on how they think their appearance is perceived by peers and how that will affect their chances in the dating game. One common occurrence during adolescence is facial acne. Acne can have a profound effect on body image and social adjustment. In a series of studies I conducted, I found that 74 percent of teenagers with moderate to severe facial acne reported that it had a damaging effect on their body image, and 43 percent indicated it had negatively affected their social lives (Cash 1995b). Their blemishes were more than skin-deep.

Sometimes the physical focus of your discontent—the chubby body, the zits, the knobby knees, or whatever—improves with time, but an emotional afterimage still burns in your private perceptions of yourself. Your body image remembers. Let me give you some examples.

In two studies (Annis, Cash, and Hrabosky 2004; Cash, Counts, and Huffine 1990), we compared the current body images of three groups: average-weight women who had never been overweight; average-weight women who had been overweight; and women currently overweight. We discovered something quite interesting—something I call "phantom fat." In many respects, currently and formerly overweight groups had a comparable body image in several (but not all) respects. However, despite the fact they had lost their excess weight, the previously overweight women had not lost the nagging feeling that their body is unacceptable. Somehow, it still felt fat, even though it wasn't anymore. At one time, they had viewed their bodies as their enemies; it's hard to forgive and forget your enemies.

This phantom fat phenomenon goes beyond matters of body weight. Evidence from my teen acne studies also confirmed that "adult survivors of adolescent acne" had a more negative body image years later as compared to their peers who had had minimal or no acne (Cash 1996). Physical scars faded, yet some emotional scars remained. Again, our body image remembers!

Bodies don't stand still. They change naturally over time. You are able to control some aspects of your appearance—for example, you can get a new hairstyle or choose what clothes to wear. But other changes are beyond your complete control. For better or worse, heredity and life events influence your looks. Take hereditary pattern hair loss for instance. Scientific research (Cash 1999) indicates that some individuals—men and women—feel helplessly unhappy about progressively thinning locks, while others just take it in stride—"hair today gone tomorrow."

People also struggle to cope with their altered appearance following traumas, such as a mastectomy or severe facial burns (Partridge 2006). These unwanted changes certainly challenge one's body image. But the inspiring fact is that many of these people come to accept such drastic changes, incorporate them into a healthy body image, and move forward in their lives (Rumsey 2002; Rumsey and Harcourt 2004, 2005).

Please appreciate the crucial point I'm conveying here: How your body appears on the outside does not have to determine how you feel on the inside. Many people who are quite short or heavy or look their elderly age or have some noticeable physical difference live enormously fulfilling lives, unaffected by what they look like. Some women become upset by their body shape changes during pregnancy; other women don't—they actually value those changes.

As some people age, they fret over wrinkles and try to erase them with expensive creams and Botox® treatments. Others age gracefully and accept physical changes as a natural fact of life. Among people born with a disfiguring condition, some agonize that they don't look "normal," yet many others have little difficulty "looking different." At the same time, do you realize that some folks whose appearance you may envy are unhappier with their looks than you might think? Your appearance doesn't mandate how you must feel. If you're faced with unwelcome changes or differences in your appearance, know that it is possible to accept these differences. *The Body Image Workbook* will teach you how to accept your body—no matter what.

DIFFERENT PERSONALITIES, DIFFERENT PATHS

The arrows of adversity aimed at us by our culture, family, or peers do not affect everyone's body image identically. Some of us have been able to transcend the ill effects of our culture's prescriptions, our peers' teasing, pimples on prom night, and even disfiguring conditions. Who are these resilient people?

They are people with solid self-esteem—they believe in themselves. Self-esteem is a powerful ally in facing and defeating life's challenges. The child, adolescent, or adult who has a secure sense of self—as being competent, lovable, and invested in hope and in living—doesn't so easily fall prey to societal "shoulds" or assaults on his or her physical worth. Self-fulfillment doesn't rely on aspirations for a perfect appearance. On the other hand, people whose nature and nurture have handed them a basic sense of inadequacy are all too eager to find fault with themselves. The infection of their inner insecurity spreads to their "outer" self.

Although poor self-esteem can pave the way for developing a negative body image, it's only a predisposition—it's not a predestination. Learning to improve body image is possible for everyone. If your self-esteem is as negative as your body image, working on improving your self-esteem can benefit your body image as well (as Danielle Lavallee and I discovered in a 1997 study).

One important personality characteristic has to do with individuals' psychological orientations to people and relationships. For example, some of us approach human relationships with enthusiasm, trust, and an expectation of enjoyment and acceptance. Others among us are more apprehensive about closeness and expect adversity or rejection, even though we may truly need just the opposite. Psychologists refer to these two orientations, respectively, as *secure* and *insecure* attachment patterns. Having a secure attachment orientation may promote a positive body image. In contrast, an insecure attachment may be a catalyst for body image insecurity to the extent that one expects or worries about the rejection of one's physical self (Cash, Theriault, and Annis 2004).

Perfectionism is another personality factor that may affect body image. There are different types of perfectionism, and the one that may be pivotal here is called *self-presentational perfectionism*. This refers to the need to present oneself to other people, in actions and appearance, as exemplary and flawless. Having this need is likely to lead to excessive investment in one's looks and concerns about being "less than perfect." One recent investigation (Rudiger et al. 2007) found that this type of perfectionism leads people to have more body image ups and downs in their day-to-day lives. Of course, the converse is also true; less perfectionism about self-presentation lowers one's vulnerability to negative body image.

Let me give you the bottom line about the people who are most resilient to threats and challenges to their body image. First and foremost, they are individuals who are protected by not being overly invested in their physical appearance for their identity or self-worth. In Step 1, they would have scored in the Acceptance Zone for body image investment (i.e., on their Appearance Importance Test). For them, looks aren't everything and don't affect everything. This doesn't mean they don't care about how they look, because they do. They enjoy looking nice, as a simple pleasure in their relationship with themselves, but not because they think of life as a beauty contest or because their worth as human beings is dictated by conforming to some societal standard of physical perfection. They keep their looks in perspective and are invested in many other things (family, friends, achievements, work, leisure interests, etc.) for self-fulfillment.

EXPERIENCING YOUR BODY IMAGE: FROM THEN TO NOW

Before we shift from the historical influences to the current causes of your body image concerns (discussed in Step 3), I want you to get in touch with your own personal body image history. I ask you to carry out the following two extremely valuable exercises to accomplish this.

Snapshots from Your Past

First, based in part on what you've just learned about the various historical causes of body image difficulties, I want you to take a few minutes to picture your body and the pertinent events and experiences that influenced your own body image development. I'm providing you with the Self-Discovery Helpsheet below to take these snapshots for specific periods of time in your life. After you complete this exercise, I'll guide you in taking more fine-grained, close-up pictures of your past.

Pictures with a Zoom Lens

On your Self-Discovery Helpsheet, you've pointed to some key events and issues in the formation of your body image. Now I want you to deeply examine those experiences that you think were especially influential. To do this, you will carry out a helpful exercise called *Expressive Writing*. Developed by Dr. James W. Pennebaker, a prominent psychologist at the University of Texas at Austin, this innovative approach helps people resolve emotionally challenging experiences (Pennebaker 2004). Scientific research on Expressive Writing has verified its therapeutic value for a range of human difficulties (Lepore and Smyth 2002; Pennebaker 1997; Pennebaker and Chung 2007).

The premise of Expressive Writing is actually quite simple. Troublesome or upsetting events may happen to us as we are growing up or during adulthood. To feel better about them, we mentally push these stressful experiences aside and try to not think about them or we forget them. The passage of time also permits the particular details to fade or become distorted. Yet the emotional aftereffects often persist, now separated from the original events that created these feelings. Sometimes these experiences even overshadow memories of events that were truly positive and satisfying during that period. As a result, we just live and react to our current feelings—disconnected from their formative history.

The purpose of Expressive Writing is *not* to ventilate or get things off your chest. Its aim is to help you create a coherent narrative that tells the meaningful story of your past experiences, along with your emotions about them. The narrative that you will write concerns your body image and the events that you believe have been influential over the course of your life. In writing your story, you will revisit the unfolding of your body image and its difficulties. You will pull together your formative body image experiences into a personally meaningful narrative.

Before you start worrying that you'll have to write an autobiographical novel, let me reassure you. You will write for only *twenty minutes each day over the next four days.* You will write in a stream of consciousness—just letting your thoughts flow, without getting bogged down with a need for correct spelling or grammar. This is not a graded assignment by an English teacher. What is essential is that your writing tells your personal story from your own viewpoint and reflects the guidelines following the Self-Discovery Helpsheet.

Self-Discovery Helpsheet:
My Body and Experiences from Then to Now

Instructions: At each period of your life listed below, what did you look like? What were the major influences on how you felt about your looks? Be sure to mention significant cultural and interpersonal influences.

Early Childhood (up to age eight)
   My Body:

   Influential Events and Experiences:

Later Childhood (age eight to puberty)
   My Body:

   Influential Events and Experiences:

Earlier Adolescence (during the physical changes of puberty to about sixteen)
   My Body:

   Influential Events and Experiences:

Later Adolescence (sixteen to twenty)
   My Body:

   Influential Events and Experiences:

Adulthood to Now
   My Body:

   Influential Events and Experiences:

- Write in the first person (say "I" and "me") and *write only for yourself*. This is not a letter and is not to be read by anyone but you. Just express yourself honestly.

- For each twenty-minute session, write at a time and in a place where you have *complete quiet and privacy*. You don't want to be interrupted by telephones ringing or by distractions from friends or family. Write *continuously* for twenty minutes without taking breaks.

- If there are topics that you aren't ready to write about yet, *don't push yourself* to do so. You can always write about them later when you are ready.

- When you write about specific events that happened, describe the events and express your *deepest thoughts and feelings*. Don't just focus on negative thoughts and feelings. To tell the whole story, include positive feelings as well.

- It is not essential to write on four consecutive days. If you need to take an occasional one-day break, that's perfectly fine. However, Expressive Writing will be most helpful if you accomplish all four sessions within a single week.

To facilitate your Expressive Writing there are two Helpsheet pages for each session. The first page gives you instructions for that session. At the end of each session, you will answer a few questions about your writing experience. Here are the Helpsheets:

Helpsheet for Change: Expressive Writing on Day 1

Instructions: On this first day of writing, write about significant body image experiences that occurred *during your childhood (before puberty)*. Express your deepest thoughts and feelings as you recall events and experiences concerning your physical appearance then. As you write, you may become aware of how these experiences connect to other feelings from that time or now—for example, feelings about yourself, about your peers, friends, or family members, or about other aspects of your life.

_____

_____

_____

_____

_____

_____

_____

_____

_____

_____

_____

_____

_____

_____

_____

_____

_____

_____

_____

_____

_____

_____

_____

_____

Helpsheet for Change: Expressive Writing on Day 1

_____

_____

_____

_____

_____

_____

_____

_____

_____

_____

_____

_____

_____

_____

_____

_____

_____

_____

_____

Use numbers from 0 = "Not at All" to 10 = "A Great Deal" to answer these questions about your expressive writing today:

1. How much did you express your deepest thoughts and feelings? _____

2. After writing today, how bothered or unhappy do you feel? _____

3. After writing today, how happy, satisfied, or at ease do you feel? _____

4. How meaningful for you was your expressive writing today? _____

Helpsheet for Change: Expressive Writing on Day 2

Instructions: On this second day of writing, write about significant body image experiences that occurred during your *early teenage years (including puberty)*. Express your deepest thoughts and feelings as you recall events and experiences concerning your physical appearance then. As you write, you may become aware of how these experiences connect to other feelings from that time or now—for example, feelings about yourself, about your peers, friends, or family members, or about other aspects of your life.

_____

_____

_____

_____

_____

_____

_____

_____

_____

_____

_____

_____

_____

_____

_____

_____

_____

_____

_____

_____

_____

_____

_____

_____

_____

_____

_____

Helpsheet for Change: Expressive Writing on Day 2

_____

_____

_____

_____

_____

_____

_____

_____

_____

_____

_____

_____

_____

_____

_____

_____

_____

_____

_____

_____

_____

_____

Use numbers from 0 = "Not at All" to 10 = "A Great Deal" to answer these questions about your expressive writing today:

1. How much did you express your deepest thoughts and feelings? _____

2. After writing today, how bothered or unhappy do you feel? _____

3. After writing today, how happy, satisfied, or at ease do you feel? _____

4. How meaningful for you was your expressive writing today? _____

Helpsheet for Change: Expressive Writing on Day 3

Instructions: On this third day of writing, write about significant body image experiences that occurred during your *mid-to-later teenage years*. Express your deepest thoughts and feelings as you recall events and experiences concerning your physical appearance then. As you write, you may become aware of how these experiences connect to other feelings from that time or now—for example, feelings about yourself, about your peers, friends, or family members, or about other aspects of your life.

_____

_____

_____

_____

_____

_____

_____

_____

_____

_____

_____

_____

_____

_____

_____

_____

_____

_____

_____

_____

_____

_____

Helpsheet for Change: Expressive Writing on Day 3

_____
_____
_____
_____
_____
_____
_____
_____
_____
_____
_____
_____
_____
_____
_____
_____
_____
_____
_____

Use numbers from 0 = "Not at All" to 10 = "A Great Deal" to answer these questions about your expressive writing today:

1. How much did you express your deepest thoughts and feelings? _____

2. After writing today, how bothered or unhappy do you feel? _____

3. After writing today, how happy, satisfied, or at ease do you feel? _____

4. How meaningful for you was your expressive writing today? _____

Helpsheet for Change: Expressive Writing on Day 4

Instructions: On this fourth and final day of writing, write about significant body image experiences that occurred *recently or in the past year or so.* Express your deepest thoughts and feelings as you describe these events and experiences. In addition, step back somewhat and try to express any insights you have about the body image issues that you've been dealing with and how they connect to other feelings or themes in your life. This is your opportunity to wrap up the story of your relationship with your body.

_____

_____

_____

_____

_____

_____

_____

_____

_____

_____

_____

_____

_____

_____

_____

_____

_____

_____

_____

_____

_____

_____

_____

_____

_____

_____

_____

_____

Helpsheet for Change: Expressive Writing on Day 4

_____

_____

_____

_____

_____

_____

_____

_____

_____

_____

_____

_____

_____

_____

_____

_____

_____

_____

_____

_____

_____

Use numbers from 0 = "Not at All" to 10 = "A Great Deal" to answer these questions about your expressive writing today:

1. How much did you express your deepest thoughts and feelings? _____

2. After writing today, how bothered or unhappy do you feel? _____

3. After writing today, how happy, satisfied, or at ease do you feel? _____

4. How meaningful for you was your expressive writing today? _____

FINAL WORDS OF ENCOURAGEMENT

Having learned about body image development and having engaged in Expressive Writing, you should now have a deeper, more coherent sense of the story of your own evolving body image. Past experiences and social conditioning can certainly program you to develop a negative body image. But history isn't everything. Understanding it differs from blaming it. Blaming your past or forces outside of your control may help you justify having a problem, but it doesn't help you solve it. Instead you conclude you are a helpless victim and you try to change nothing.

The current causes are especially important; that is, the here-and-now factors that affect your body image experiences in everyday life. These influences can propagate and reinforce your personal body image struggles, or they can extricate you from your past programming. If past conditioning was all-powerful, achieving a positive body image would be practically impossible. Most people find ways to transcend the nasty lessons of the past and accept their overall appearance, despite real or perceived physical imperfections. So can you!

Change will occur if you begin to take responsibility for the choices you make today. After all, today is tomorrow's history, and that's history you can do something about. Taking responsibility for change starts with a two simple realizations: First, you feel what you think. Your judgments and interpretations of events, not the events themselves, govern your emotional experiences. Second, how you mentally and behaviorally react to your thoughts and feelings can either make things worse or make them better. Step 3 will empower you take this responsibility for acceptance of your inner experiences and your body.

Mindfully Accepting Your Body Image Experiences

In your everyday life, probably lots of things trigger your thoughts, feelings, images, memories, expectations, intentions, and other private experiences concerning what you look like. Some of these inner experiences are distracting, annoying, upsetting, or even painful. But you may take them very seriously and treat them as truths or realities. You may see them as defining who you are as a person. Most likely, you want to get rid of these inner experiences, so you probably react by trying to avoid them or whatever sets them off. You take "corrective actions" to try to change or camouflage how you look, hoping to escape your inner pain.

EXPERIENCES

Consider Joyce's body image experiences: Whenever she thinks about her figure, she gets a sinking, hopeless feeling deep down inside. She is repulsed by the size of her thighs and hips. Whenever her fiancé, Jeff, catches a glimpse of her as she emerges naked from the shower, at first Joyce feels intensely self-conscious. Then, she quickly cloaks her body in a towel and is flooded with embarrassment and makes up an excuse to banish him from the bathroom. Her embarrassment gives way to shame and then becomes anger. She is angry that Jeff saw her body so closely, and even angrier with her body for the betrayal.

Joyce also routinely locks the bedroom door to get dressed privately, so Jeff won't see her body. She becomes terribly frustrated as she tries to find the "right outfit" to conceal the curves of her hips and thighs. The struggle to dress to conceal her body is one version of the emotional roller coaster that Joyce rides daily, without amusement. From many painful experiences like these, Joyce has concluded she is both ugly and a "hopelessly messed-up" person.

THE PIVOTAL POWER OF NOW: THE EYES OF THE BEHOLDER BELONG TO YOU

At the end of Step 2, I explained that the most important causes of body image problems exist in the here and now. Specifically, your body image emotions are driven by your thoughts. The often subtle and unspoken messages you give yourself—your assumptions, perceptions, and interpretations—decisively dictate your feelings about your looks. Your patterns of relating and interacting with yourself produce a negative body image. You create your own conditioning. Although the seeds of body image distress may have been planted in your cultural and interpersonal history, a negative body image exists and grows in the presence of your mind.

Right now, in the here and now, I want to ask you to try something: I want you to think about the aspect of your appearance you like least. Picture it clearly in your mind's eye. Now think these thoughts about this attribute: "It looks awful. Ugly. It's really ugly. I hate it. I really hate it. Everybody hates looking at it. People think I'm ugly. I'm really, really ugly." After saying these things to yourself, over and over, for one entire minute, check your feelings.

For many people, this little exercise gives rise to extremely unhappy body image feelings. After only one minute of immersing your mind in such self-critical thinking, you start feeling homely and hopeless. Did this one-minute exercise have a familiar ring to it?

Let me further illustrate the pivotal power of human thought by describing an eye-opening experiment conducted by psychologists at Dartmouth University (Kleck and Strenta 1980). The investigators used theatrical makeup to create a facial scar on their research participants before they were to interact face-to-face with a stranger. The stranger worked for the researchers and had been trained to act in a standard neutral way with each subject. What the participants didn't know, however, was the hideous scar had actually been removed before their conversation with the stranger. After the conversation, they were asked questions about how the stranger had related to them.

Compared to the control group, who had not been given a "scar," the participants who *believed* they had the facial scar "witnessed" more discomfort in the stranger's behavior—such as staring at them or avoiding looking at them at all. They reported experiencing the self-conscious and adverse effects of their facial "flaw," even though no flaw existed. Obviously, since there was no actual scar, these people created their own reality. Their experiences reflected what they believed about their looks, not the objective facts of the situation.

This fascinating experiment demonstrates a profoundly important truth: The most influential dictators of negative body image emotions are your own ways of judging and thinking about your looks. Many of your thought patterns may have become so automatic and habitual that you're not even conscious of them as they occur. Specific events may trigger these thoughts, but once they start up, the emotional damage follows, which breeds more self-critical ruminations and, in turn, even greater despair. Then, to cope with your self-inflicted distress, you may avoid those people or situations that triggered

Figure 3.1
Body Image Experiences: Here-and-Now Influences

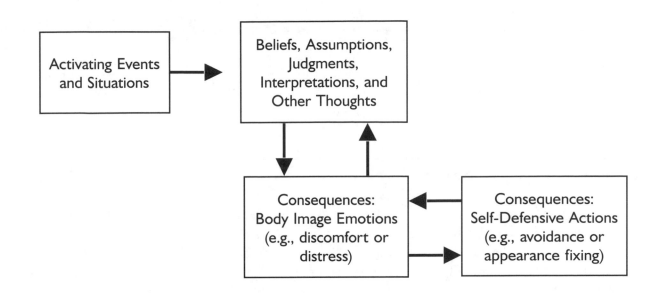

your cascade of negative thoughts and feelings. Or, you may carry out time-consuming rituals in which you try to fix or hide the "flaws" in your appearance. Obviously, these self-protective efforts don't fix your long-standing body image problems. In fact, they provide only temporary relief and actually perpetuate your problems.

In Step 2, you learned and wrote about historical factors that predisposed you to create negative body image experiences. Figure 3.1 is an informative flow diagram of the here-and-now causes of a negative body image. It shows the vicious cycle of self-defeating thoughts, emotions, and behaviors. When you develop a different mind-set that breaks this cycle, it becomes possible to overcome a negative body image. You can learn to change your experiences—how you think, act, and feel—now and in the future.

The Body Image Workbook will help you do this, so that your old painful patterns give way as you discover new and satisfying ways to experience your body and yourself.

WHAT IS MINDFULNESS?

Throughout your work with *The Body Image Workbook*, you will cultivate a new mind-set that greatly differs from how you currently think, feel, and act. This new mind-set is one of *mindfulness* and *acceptance*. Put most simply, mindfulness is a way of directing attention or awareness. It is a way of consciously and purposefully "stepping back" and observing your inner experiences in the here and now. Far from being new or modern, mindfulness has been a part of Eastern psychological and philosophical (especially Buddhist) perspectives for centuries. Mindfulness is a central facet of many (but not all) approaches to meditation. Becoming mindful certainly doesn't require converting to a particular religious doctrine. It simply means being open to and practicing a novel mind-set.

In recent years, mindfulness has become innovatively integrated into Western approaches to psychotherapy and human growth (e.g., Baer, 2006; Germer, Siegel, and Fulton 2005; Hayes, Follette, and Linehan 2004; Kabat-Zinn 1994; Segal, Williams, and Teasdale 2002). Of course, given the Western commitment to science, mindfulness-based approaches have been subjected to much scientific scrutiny, and they've been found to provide valuable and enhanced benefits in health promotion and the reduction of psychological suffering (e.g., Hayes, Follette, and Linehan 2004; Marra 2005). I believe that a more mindful orientation toward your body image experiences holds great promise for you.

WHAT IS ACCEPTANCE?

Acceptance means seeing things as they really are and seeing them in the present moment. A stomachache is a stomachache and it hurts. Feeling anxious or self-conscious or sad or mad are just what they are—your feelings of the moment. Not liking your body in some situation is simply what it is, nothing more and nothing less. Currently, you judge your negative body image experiences. From Step 2 of this program, you've learned how these experiences and your judgments of them came about. In judging, you reach four verdicts:

1. The first verdict equates thoughts and feelings with truth. When you think or feel that you're "ugly" or "fat" or physically "unacceptable," you judge these experiences as a valid indictment of your body and your self-worth. Of course, they are only thoughts and feelings. They are not evidence of any truth. Acceptance means recognizing that your experiences are merely inner events. You can be objectively aware of these events and see them for what they truly are—just inner thoughts and feelings.

2. The second judgmental verdict deems your inner experiences as intolerable. You judge them by concluding, "I can't handle feeling this way" (self-consciousness, shame, or anxiety). Acceptance means being mindfully aware of your emotional discomfort and seeing it as familiar and as just discomfort.

3. From the first two verdicts, the third concludes that you must do something or must not do something so that you might escape or avoid this "intolerable" experience. You tell yourself to avoid a threatening situation, to modify your appearance in some way, and/or do something else to "fix this." Mindful acceptance just witnesses your habitual impulses for self-protective action, but it doesn't require your action. Instead, you objectively observe your impulsive wishes or intentions as internal experiences, as "voices in your head." You notice your inner voices and hear what they are commanding that you do or not do, but you *don't* follow their commands. You simply become aware of them as your experiences.

4. The fourth verdict involves your indictment of yourself as "sick," "screwed up," "hopeless," or "a worthless person" for having the above-described experiences. You don't accept the experiences and cannot accept yourself if you have them. With the practice of mindful acceptance, you come to see that you give yourself a hard time for having a hard time. You recognize what you are doing—that you add this additional self-loathing layer to your experience. Your indictment of yourself is not evidence of the truth of your negative thoughts. It is only an additional inner voice.

Having emotions, including painful emotions, is characteristically human. Emotions can serve as important, potentially adaptive signals to get our attention to process information about something that's happening. When we reflexively seek to turn off the emotion instead of becoming more aware of it, a problem occurs. Another problem arises if we engage in self-defensive maneuvers to prevent our experiencing the emotion in the future. Such efforts, called *Experiential Avoidance,* turn us against our own mind and against ourselves. Attempts to deny, disregard, deflect, or defend against discomfort ultimately create profound psychological suffering. The suffering is especially intense if we loathe ourselves for our own humanity.

LEARNING ABOUT MINDFULNESS AND ACCEPTANCE

I suspect that my explanations of mindfulness and acceptance may leave you somewhat puzzled or doubtful. That's absolutely okay. Just be mindful of your uncertainty and accept it for what it is—your experience of uncertainty. Be aware of your inner reactions. Are you confused? Are you skeptical? Are you thinking, "He's trying to tell me I'm not really ugly"? Are you thinking, "I wish I could be more mindful and accepting"? You need not do anything about your reactions, except to be aware of them and accept them as your reactions at the moment. But please keep reading. To begin to discover mindfulness, allow yourself to experience three exercises recommended by mindfulness and acceptance experts (i.e., Hayes and Smith 2005; Kabat-Zinn 1990, 1994).

Raisin Your Awareness

If you ever eat raisins (or popcorn or nuts), have you noticed that you just pop some into your mouth, munch them a few times, swallow, and open your mouth to repeat these actions? You may do this mindlessly because you are simultaneously doing something else, like having a conversation, reading, or watching television or a movie. So now, I ask you to get some raisins and do this differently. Spend at least one minute with each step below:

1. Put one raisin in your palm and look at it closely. Notice its wrinkles and crevices and the shapes they form. Notice its color and any slight variations in color.

2. Put a second raisin in your palm next to the first. Notice how they look alike. Notice how they look different.

3. Roll one of the raisins continuously between your thumb and index finger. Notice how what you just saw now feels. Feel the crevices. Feel the softness and the hardness and the stickiness.

4. Put the raisin into your mouth, but don't bite into it. Roll it around, feeling with your tongue what you just felt with your fingers. Notice its texture. As you move it around in your mouth, be aware of how it feels in different places in your mouth.

5. Now, bite down once on the raisin. Notice its taste. Bite down again. Notice its changing texture. Swallow it and stay aware of the sensation of the raisin as it slides down your throat.

6. Place the second raisin in your mouth and chew it very slowly. As you keep chewing, notice as the raisin's consistency becomes mushy and then even mushier. Take note of how this raisin feels in comparison to the first one. Swallow it when you wish.

How did this compare with your usual experience of eating raisins?

Body Scan

Because your experiences of your body are troubling to you, this second exercise is a really important one. You often live in your body as if it were an "esthetic object"—something that is looked at only from the outside. Now, I encourage you to experience your body mindfully from the inside. Here's how to do that:

1. First, choose a quiet, private, and comfortable place to lie down. Make sure you will not be distracted by the phone, television, bright lighting, or interruptions from friends or family. Once there, lie down on your back and allow your eyes to gently close.

2. Simply become aware of your breathing as you slowly inhale and exhale. Notice your stomach rising and falling with each breath.

3. Then, simply become aware of sensations from your body as a whole. Notice how your body feels. Notice how it feels where it touches your clothing, where it touches the surface beneath you.

4. Focus on the toes of your left foot. Be aware of how they feel. As you pay attention to them, see if you can transfer your experience of breathing to them, as if you are breathing *into* your toes and breathing out *from* your toes. Just imagine the sensations of your breathing moving downward from your nose first to your belly and then to your toes. Just focus on the sensations of this breathing into your toes. Allow yourself to experience this. If you cannot, just be aware that this is not your experience. That's okay. Not having these sensations is your real experience. There's nothing to judge.

5. Slowly move on, transferring the sensations of breathing in and out to another part of your body, followed by another part, and then another, as you move the flow of your breathing and your awareness to specific areas throughout your body.

The aim of the body scan is to mindfully experience in the present whatever occurs. It's not a test. It is a valuable opportunity for you to learn to be mindful and to accept whatever your experiences are, without judging them. I strongly encourage you to give yourself a full or partial body scan for about twenty to thirty minutes a day for at least a couple of weeks. You will see that your capacity for mindfulness will grow. Ultimately, you'll see how this capacity can contribute to your acceptance of your body "on the outside."

Be Mindful of Minutiae

You can cultivate mindfulness as you carry out routine chores and tasks in your daily life. These are the things we most often do mindlessly, because they are so familiar or habitual they are on "automatic" and require no thought. Here are some examples:

- Sitting and standing
- Walking around a room, in random directions
- Climbing and descending stairs
- Taking a shower
- Brushing your teeth
- Sweeping the floor
- Drinking a glass of water
- Petting your cat or dog
- Dressing and undressing
- Cooking
- Eating
- Washing dishes
- Listening to music
- Gardening
- Walking in the rain
- Making love

By doing these activities mindfully, you will stay focused in the present and on your mental and sensory experiences. If your attention drifts elsewhere, don't judge it. This is what minds do. They wander. So just notice it and then bring your attention back to the activity.

These three exercises are just a small sample of ways that you can begin to help yourself create a life of mindfulness and acceptance. Later, in Step 6 of this workbook, you'll learn Body-and-Mind Relaxation exercises that can further enhance your mindful acceptance of your experiences. If you're curious, take a peek at Learning Body-and-Mind Relaxation in that chapter. Moreover, in the Recommended Resources section at the end of this workbook, you will find some terrific books filled with useful insights and exercises for the enhancement of mindfulness and acceptance.

Right now, I want to introduce a very special activity. It enables you to begin to directly apply mindfulness and acceptance to your body image.

MIRROR REFLECTIONS

I once conducted a research survey and asked people, "What do you see when you look in the mirror?" Here are excerpts from some poignant "reflections":

What I see I really hate. I hate my thighs. I hate my butt. My mouth is too big. My hair is too straight. I wish I didn't have to spend so much time on my looks. Tomorrow, I'll start working out. (white woman, age twenty-five)

What I see is a body I regret to call my own. I wasn't fond of it as a child. I really disliked it as a teenager. My adult years have been filled with constant contempt of my ugly fat body. I would trade it in for almost anything else. (white man, age forty-five)

I see a slim, healthy-looking woman, until I look into her eyes. What am I going to do about these bags growing under my eyes? I look pretty good for thirty-two. But what will I see when I'm fifty or sixty? Perish the thought! (white woman, age thirty-two)

I see an average-looking dude. I wish I was bigger. I wish my hair was thicker. I wish I was a couple of inches taller. Why am I kidding myself? I'm less than an average-looking dude. I'd settle for average. (African-American man, age twenty-six)

I see an old fart. How and when did this happen? (white man, age sixty-three)

I see a tall, well-built young man who has a crippling injury of his right hand. If it weren't for my deformity, I'd be the happiest guy in the world. (white man, age nineteen)

I see a gal who looks pretty good. Just don't ask her to take her clothes off. Then you'll get another story. But I'll spare you the ugly details. (Hispanic woman, age forty-one)

I see a woman who looks like a girl. If it weren't for my big nipples I'd have no breasts at all. (white woman, age thirty-one)

I see a fairly attractive young lady who can't stop thinking about the things that keep her from being a very attractive young lady. (white woman, age twenty-eight)

I see a skinny guy with a receding hairline and acne scars. I see a loser!
(Hispanic man, age thirty-one)

What I try to see (but can't) is what I dream about being: Rich! Rich enough to afford plastic surgery on my nose, to have my teeth fixed plus a chin implant, to have my makeup and hair done professionally. Then, there are the fashionable clothes. Dream on! I'm always going to be a plain Jane. (white woman, age thirty-three)

I see a short girl with an hourglass figure, but the sand has all settled on the bottom.
(white woman, age nineteen)

All I see is a guy in a wheelchair with skinny legs. Unfortunately, I know that's all everybody else sees too. (Asian man, age forty-eight)

I see that I need to lose weight. My arms are covered with dark hair that I'm always hiding or bleaching. Why can't I be as pretty as other girls? (white woman, age twenty-two)

When I look in the mirror, I see nothing. That's because I'm too scared to open my eyes. Sorry.
(Pacific Islander woman, age nineteen)

I see zits and fat cheeks. Yuck! (white woman, age nineteen)

Mirror, mirror on the wall, who's the fairest of them all? It ain't me, babe!
(Hispanic woman, age thirty-eight)

Your Current Mirror Reflections

So what do you see when you look in the mirror? Before learning how to apply mindfulness and acceptance, first answer this question based on your characteristic experience of looking at yourself in the mirror. Spend about five minutes privately viewing your reflection in a full-length mirror. Please do this without being overly clothed. For example, even though it may be a bit uncomfortable, view yourself while wearing only your underclothes, after you've taken a bath or shower. Be mindful of what you are looking at, the thoughts that pass through your head, and the emotions you are aware of. Use the following Self-Discovery Helpsheet to record this experience.

Your Mindful Mirror Reflections

If you are like many people, your experience of looking at your reflection in the mirror is probably biased, judgmental, and mindless. It is biased to the extent that you focus on some aspects of your physical self and not others. A negative body image leads you to focus on "what's wrong" with your looks—what you have the strongest concerns about. These are your body image hot spots. Your bias

Self-Discovery Helpsheet: Reflections in My Mirror

What do you see when you look in the mirror?

_____

_____

_____

_____

_____

_____

What thoughts run through your mind as you view your reflection?

_____

_____

_____

_____

_____

_____

What emotional reactions do you have as you look at your reflection?

_____

_____

_____

_____

_____

_____

also means that you have blind spots, which are the facets of your appearance that you neglect to focus on in the mirror.

Your experience is also likely to be judgmental. You don't merely observe. You evaluate, and you do so critically. Your inner thoughts may use harsh words. You say "fat" or "ugly" or "gross" or other words similar to those of many of the people I quoted earlier in this chapter. Understandably, this can be a very emotional experience that triggers discomfort, disgust, or despair. Maybe you compare what you see with what you wish you saw. Maybe this leads to thoughts about how you could "fix" what you see, by changing your body or concealing certain aspects of your body. Maybe you leave the present to recall past disappointments with your body or jump to the future and make predictions about what might happen because of how you are judging your looks. Maybe these judgments and uncomfortable emotions lead you to want to avoid looking at yourself and cause you to retreat from the mirror.

Finally, the experience is likely to be a mindless one. You are not merely standing back and objectively observing your thoughts and feelings. You are reacting to them. You are in your mind and not "out of your mind." You are not controlling your mind; rather, it is controlling you.

Now it's time to apply mindfulness and acceptance in an exercise of looking at your reflection in the mirror. This is not a silly little assignment. It is a very important opportunity to begin to change how you experience your body. In fact, scientific studies have verified that this exercise can produce meaningful improvements in those with body image problems (e.g., Delinsky and Wilson 2006; Hilbert, Tuschen-Caffier, and Vögele 2002; Key et al. 2002). What makes this "mirror exposure" experience especially significant and helpful is that it actually represents a microcosm of your body image experiences in your daily life. Therefore the exercise is an excellent training ground in developing a new mind-set that you can carry with you everywhere—even beyond the mirror.

I'll guide you step-by-step through Mindful Mirror Reflections. Let's do this in four sessions, each separated by one day. Allow about twenty minutes for each session. After each session, use the Helpsheet for Change that follows to summarize your experiences.

Mindful Mirror Reflections

SESSION 1

- Use a full-length mirror where you have complete privacy and won't be interrupted. Dress as you normally do.

- Stand in front of the mirror and for two minutes look at your reflection from head to toe. Rather than zooming in on hot spots or ignoring blind spots, I want you to look at each area of your body. View your body from the front, side, and back.

- Then, from head to toe describe each aspect or feature of your body. Describe it *out loud*. Describe it as you would to a blind person who wants to know what you look like, or to an artist who is sketching you without seeing you.

- Be objectively descriptive, not evaluative or judgmental. Include descriptions of color, texture, size, shape, symmetry, etc. Do not use subjectively critical or exaggerating words ("ugly face," "gross," "dumpy," "scrawny legs," "bad hair," "beady eyes," "fat ass," and so forth). If you become aware that you expressed a judgment or criticism, pause to look at the feature again and use a more objective, factual term.

- Continue to look at your body from all angles. If there are areas or features you are aware of that you left out, describe them objectively and nonjudgmentally.

- Complete your session by spending a minute silently looking at your total reflection, your body as a whole and not as parts.

- During this session, be aware of any feelings you experience at the moment that you are viewing and describing a particular feature. Just notice your feelings and briefly describe them aloud (e.g., "I am feeling happy" or "I am feeling anxious"). Then simply shift your attention to the next area you will describe objectively.

SESSION 2

- Repeat everything you did in Session 1. This time move from toe to head, instead of from head to toe, and again view your body from the front, side, and back. Be sure to attend to both hot spots and blind spots.

- At the end, spend three minutes silently looking at your body as a whole, not as parts.

SESSIONS 3 AND 4

- In these two sessions, you will do exactly what you did in Sessions 1 and 2, except that you will dress differently. Wear more revealing attire so that you can see more of your own skin. Ideally, you would be wearing only your underwear. If you are too uncomfortable to do so at this point, then wear shorts and a snug, sleeveless top.

- In Session 3, you'll wear less and follow the instructions for Session 1.

- In Session 4, you'll wear less and follow the instructions for Session 2.

Helpsheet for Change: Mindful Mirror Reflections

Describe your experiences of each session. How did it feel? What did you learn?

Session 1: _____

_____

_____

_____

_____

_____

Session 2: _____

_____

_____

_____

_____

_____

Session 3: _____

_____

_____

_____

_____

_____

Session 4: _____

_____

_____

_____

_____

_____

UNDERSTANDING YOUR BODY IMAGE IN EVERYDAY LIFE

In Step 1, you summarized your self-discoveries in your personal Body Image Profile. It highlights how you generally think, feel, and act in regard to your body image. However, each occurrence, or episode, of body image distress has its own unique elements—specific thoughts, emotions, and behaviors—that unfold in reaction to particular situations and events. Changing your body image requires that you examine and understand the specifics of each distressing episode as it takes place. This is possible when you keep a special diary that works like a videotape recording the moment-to-moment expression of your body image.

I will teach you how to successfully monitor your experiences and record them in your Body Image Diary. This will build on your Mindful Mirror Reflections exercises. The primary purpose of self-monitoring and diary-keeping is to facilitate your mindful understanding and acceptance of your body image thoughts and feelings and how they unfold and affect you from day to day. This kind of self-discovery is a helpful catalyst for body image acceptance and is supported by research (Cash and Hrabosky 2003).

Mindful Self-Monitoring

One basic tenet of most psychological therapies is that people can solve their personal problems if they can learn to examine their own minds and actions with objectivity and accuracy. If you no longer want to be controlled by negative emotions, you must be able to step back from your subjective experience and ask yourself the following fundamental questions:

- What am I feeling?

- What just happened to lead me to feel this way?

- What am I saying to myself in this situation?

- How am I reacting (or wanting to react) behaviorally to this experience?

Asking and answering these questions reflects a powerful process called *mindful self-monitoring*. Self-monitoring is analogous to eavesdropping on yourself. You become consciously attuned to specific aspects of your own ongoing experience. You observe precisely what is going on. When body image feelings occur, you identify what emotions you're having. You pinpoint what's happened in the situation that has triggered these emotions. You listen objectively to the thoughts and perceptions that are running through your mind. You also monitor how you behave in reaction to these thoughts and emotions.

Mindful self-monitoring is a skill, and skills can only develop through practice. Most people with a negative body image focus only on being upset and on blaming their appearance for their unhappiness. They just feel what they feel and do what they do. They react reflexively and never step back to dissect their experience objectively.

Plenty of people respond to the notion of self-monitoring by claiming they already do it and it doesn't help. They say, "I'm always analyzing my looks. I'm always focusing on how crummy I feel about my body." Being intensely aware of your appearance or deeply immersed in emotion is *not* self-monitoring—it's actually part of the problem you want to change.

To change, you must develop a more objective view of your experiences. If you've loathed your looks for many years, it's difficult to separate the self-hatred from whatever it is about your appearance that you hate. Besides, if you've persuaded yourself that your body is the problem, then your body image miseries will seem justified. You argue, "My awful looks make me feel awful." In time, you'll see that you're wrong, so bear with me. With time and practice, you can become open, observant, and objective enough to monitor reality and change your self-hating or negative body image experiences.

EPISODES

Some people insist that they don't have episodes of body image distress. When the concept is explained to them, all they see is that "life is one big, nonstop episode." Allow me to explain what I mean by an episode. Although you may "always" dislike your nose, your weight, your pear shape, or any other physical attribute, you aren't constantly thinking about it, nor are you continually upset about it. Like a sleeping dragon, your discontent is sometimes dormant; other times it breathes fire and belches smoke. Something happens to rouse your dissatisfaction. Then, as you dwell on that something, your emotions are aroused and become especially negative and intense. These particularly troublesome times that enter your consciousness are what I mean by *body image episodes*.

Learning Your Body Image ABCs

You probably have experienced some episodes that repeat themselves like a broken record. If that is the case, take some time to recollect several recent episodes of body image distress, particularly ones that you expect to recur. You will identify three elements of each episode and record them in your Body Image Diary. The following three elements make up the *ABC Sequence*. They are derived from figure 3.1, depicting your here-and-now body image experiences:

1. **A** stands for the Activators. What events activated or triggered your feelings about your looks? In your diary, you'll write down a brief, specific description of the situation and occurrences that immediately preceded your distress.

2. **B** stands for your Beliefs—your thoughts about and interpretations of the activating events that were going through your mind at the time. Replay the tape—the mental conversation you were having with yourself. How were you viewing the situation? What were you saying to yourself about the events? Recalling your thoughts out of their actual context can be difficult. Remind yourself by filling in the blank: "I was thinking _____," or "I was probably thinking _____."

3. **C** stands for the Consequences of your thoughts and beliefs. How did you react emotionally? How did you react behaviorally?

In your Body Image Diary, you will describe the Consequences in terms of the *TIDE* of the episode. TIDE is an acronym to help you analyze the four essential aspects of consequences that occur:

1. **T** stands for the Type of emotion you felt in the situation. Self-consciousness? Anxiety? Anger? Depression? Shame? Disgust? Envy? Embarrassment? A mixture of emotions? Identify the feeling or feelings that you had.

2. **I** stands for the Intensity of your emotions. Rate their strength at their peak, from 0 for "not at all intense" to 10 for "extremely intense."

3. **D** stands for the episode's Duration. How long did your distress last? About how many minutes or hours did it take before you felt noticeably better?

4. **E** represents the Effects of the episode on your behavior. Your actions at this point are often reflexive efforts to cope with or defend yourself against your unwanted emotions. Did you try to get out of the situation? Did you become sullen and withdraw? Did you attempt to fix or conceal the part of your physical self that you were bothered about? Did you take your feelings out on others? Did you take them out on yourself?

The more types of emotions you feel with greater intensity for a longer duration and with more behavioral effects, the more powerful the episode—like being caught up in a turbulent TIDE.

HOW TO KEEP YOUR BODY IMAGE DIARY

A personal Body Image Diary is an essential tool for learning to deal with your body image difficulties and to accept your looks. The Helpsheet for Change at the end of this chapter shows the format for monitoring, dissecting, and recording the ABC Sequences of your negative body image episodes. Just write out the format of the diary in a personal notebook. (This may be more convenient than photocopying the Helpsheet and having lots of unbound sheets of paper to keep up with.)

Retrospective Self-Monitoring

Because your negative body image emotions may interfere with learning to self-monitor, let's start off by monitoring experiences from your recent past. Soon you'll be able to use your new ability right in the middle of an upsetting body image episode. So, now, I'll ask you to do three things:

1. First, to see how to record an episode in the Body Image Diary, examine the two sample diary entries that precede the blank Body Image Diary page that you will use as the format to record your own body image experiences.

2. Then, go back to Step 1 and review your answers to the Body Image Distress Test and the Body Image Thoughts Test. This will remind you of your Activators and your Beliefs that produce your own troublesome Consequences.

3. To become skilled in identifying your body image ABCs, complete your Body Image Diary for five or more recent, past episodes. For each, mentally recreate the experience. Close your eyes and picture the situation. Replay your mental tape of the episode—the triggering events and your thoughts, emotions, and actions.

After analyzing the ABC Sequence and Emotional TIDE of past episodes, you'll be ready for current, up-to-date self-monitoring.

Here-and-Now Self-Monitoring

For at least four or five days, monitor any episode as it occurs. Apply what you've learned about mindfulness and acceptance in this Step. Just observe the ABCs as they unfold. Be aware of the situational events that activate your inner experiences. Don't try to change the episode. Just let it flow and observe your experiences without judging them. Listen to the thoughts you have as if they were the dialogue from a movie you are watching. Attend to your emotions. What are they? How strong are they? What do you do or want to do in reaction to these thoughts and feelings?

Afterward, as soon as possible, make a Body Image Diary entry.

FINAL WORDS OF ENCOURAGEMENT

Acquiring a mindful and accepting perspective on your body image experiences doesn't magically happen overnight. You should integrate what you've learned in this chapter into your life. Please repeat and practice the various exercises so that they can become a part of you. Keep using your Body Image Diary each day so that you can become more and more mindful, not only of how these experiences flow but also of how they are changing.

To conclude Step 3, I want to share with you a Buddhist saying that captures the essence of this Step:

> *The secret of health for both mind and body is*
> *Not to mourn for the past, not to worry about the future,*
> *And not to anticipate troubles,*
> *But to live in the present moment wisely and earnestly.*

I also wish to share the titles of some very useful books that will enlighten and help you create a life (and body image) of mindfulness and acceptance. For these titles, please refer to the Recommended Resources section of this book. For additional resources for the material covered in Step 3, look in the Mindfulness and Acceptance listings. And I encourage you to go online to learn more about these and other resources.

Helpsheet for Change: Sample Body Image Diary for Carole

Date: *July 20*

ABC Sequence of My Body Image Experiences

Activators (Triggering events and situations): *Attended a pool party where I had to wear a swimsuit and eat lunch in front of others—especially guys.*

Beliefs (Thoughts and interpretations about my appearance and myself):
I kept thinking I looked fat and flabby compared to the other girls there. I wished I could be invisible. I wondered what guys were thinking about how I looked. I thought they were "totally grossed out." I thought if they saw me eat anything they'd really notice I was fat. I kept thinking that I had to lose weight soon.

Consequences (Emotional TIDE):

Types of emotions: *Anxiety, self-consciousness, and despair; angry with myself.*

Intensity of emotions (0 to 10): *9*

Duration of the episode: *For the entire time I was there (4 hours)*

Effects of the episode on my behavior: *I got quiet and didn't talk much with anybody except Sharon, my best friend. I didn't eat anything (but did drink too much wine). I didn't go in the pool. Just kept a towel around me most of the time. I made Sharon leave with me before the party was over.*

Helpsheet for Change: Sample Body Image Diary for Larry

Date: *February 4*

ABC Sequence of My Body Image Experiences

Activators (Triggering events and situations): *Making out in bed with my girlfriend, Jessica.*

Beliefs (Thoughts and interpretations about my appearance and myself):
As usual, very distracted by thoughts about how my body isn't muscular enough. Kept thinking she was wishing I was better built and was secretly turned off. I was worried that she might touch me in places that are skinny or bony. Kept thinking about how to get out of this situation.

Consequences (Emotional TIDE):

Types of emotions: *Anxiety, shame, and self-consciousness; felt guilty for disappointing her.*

Intensity of emotions (0 to 10): *5*

Duration of the episode: *15 minutes*

Effects of the episode on my behavior: *I was fidgety and quickly lost my interest in having sex so I stopped. I "fibbed"—told Jessica I had a sore back from working out. Left the room to go check e-mails and tried not to think about this.*

Helpsheet for Change: Sample Body Image Diary for _____

Date: _____

ABC Sequence of My Body Image Experiences

Activators (Triggering events and situations):

_____

_____

_____

_____

Beliefs (Thoughts and interpretations about my appearance and myself):

_____

_____

_____

_____

Consequences (Emotional TIDE):

Types of emotions: _____

Intensity of emotions (0 to 10): _____

Duration of the episode: _____

Effects of the episode on my behavior:

_____

_____

_____

_____

Seeing Beneath the Surface of Your Private Body Talk

Are you talking to yourself again? Of course you are! We all talk to ourselves in the privacy of our own minds. This is called an *internal dialogue*, or mental conversation. Your silent dialogues consist of thoughts that reflect your perceptions and interpretations of actual or potential events in your life. These mental conversations also include *self-statements*—thoughts and inferences or conclusions about yourself. Your emotions flow from how you talk to yourself about yourself. Step 3 should have helped you become increasingly attuned to your internal conversations.

Your inner discourse often happens without you realizing that you're talking to yourself. These mental processes are so ingrained that they occur automatically. They are not intentional, conscious thought. This habitual, automatic-pilot mode of thought just happens and, in a sense, is mindless—because you aren't aware of or thinking about your thinking.

Among the obvious liabilities of mindlessness is the fact that you don't know your own mind. You don't see the crucial connections between your silent assumptions, thoughts, and interpretations and how you feel and act. Usually you notice only the emotions that these dialogues generate. So, you end up having to deal with all of these feelings, especially if they are negative and intense. Rarely do you reverse your mental tape and listen closely and objectively to the inner conversations that led you astray. But that's exactly what must be done.

THE VOICES WITHIN: YOUR PRIVATE BODY TALK

To overcome your body image difficulties, you must first become mindfully aware of your inner conversations, especially those that deal with your physical appearance. I call these internal dialogues your *Private*

Body Talk. Fortunately, you're already in training. For a while, since you finished Step 3, you've been monitoring and keeping a diary of the ABC Sequence of your body image experiences—the Activators, Beliefs, and Consequences of those experiences. You've begun to observe and accept your thoughts and feelings as they are, rather than treating them as ultimate truths or something you must avoid. What happens during the B stage will influence your emotional responses to the activating events. It will also affect how you try to defend yourself against your uncomfortable emotions. Of course, B is the part of your mind where your Private Body Talk takes place—where biased, irrational, and self-defeating conversations occur.

Let me illustrate how crucial different styles of Private Body Talk can be: Kerri and Sherri are identical twins. One day, they're together in the dressing room at a health club. After working out, both are in a pretty good mood. Before leaving, each looks at herself in the mirror for a few moments. Afterward, Kerri leaves feeling bummed out and down on herself. Sherri, on the other hand, walks away feeling particularly upbeat and confident about herself. Given that these two women look exactly alike, we must wonder what happened here.

What happened was the Private Body Talk that each twin had with herself while looking at her reflection in the mirror. Kerri's Private Body Talk said "Oh God, I look so ugly. I absolutely detest the way I look. I'm fat. If I don't lose ten pounds, nobody will ever be attracted to me. I hate my face. Look at my stupid fleshy cheeks. Everybody who knows me thinks I'm repulsive." No wonder Kerri walked away from the mirror (and her Private Body Talk) feeling miserable and wishing she could crawl into a hole and hide.

In spite of the fact that they are identical twins, Sherri's Private Body Talk was hardly identical: Her Private Body Talk went like this, "Gee, I look kind of nice today. I really like this new lip gloss. It makes me want to smile, which shows my nice teeth. This blue shirt accentuates the blue in my eyes. I love blue. I'd like to lose a few pounds, but my life won't end if I don't. Besides, my body really feels energized from my workout today and I feel great."

Whose Private Body Talk sounds more like yours? Like Kerri, do you torture yourself with a stream of malicious remarks and dire predictions? How derogatory are the dialogues that you've recorded in your diary? To change your self-demeaning Private Body Talk, you must ask another important question: "Why do I do this to myself? Why do I carry on such self-disparaging dialogues in the first place?"

I'll tell you why. To do that, let's go back to the twins and ask this question: Why did Sherri have an inner conversation that gave her confidence and cheerfulness, while Kerri's Private Body Talk had nothing nice to say and made her miserable? You might guess that their parents or peers may have interacted more favorably with Sherri than with her sister. Perhaps some people somehow preferred her and praised her looks more. Maybe it stemmed from when she was six years old and their daddy nicknamed her "my little chipmunk." Maybe she had a more bothersome bout with teen acne than Sherri did. Maybe Kerri used to have a boyfriend who badgered her to shed weight because he "liked the cheerleader look."

Maybe, maybe, maybe … you could go on forever guessing about the differences in the twins' personal histories that forged different Private Body Talk. You'd probably be right in some of your speculations. It's true that disturbing events can have a lasting effect on your body image and how you think about yourself. I suspect that you wrote about some of these personal experiences in Step 2 of the workbook. Such unfortunate events may have taught you something—something that fed upon itself and remains with you still. This "something" drives your negative Private Body Talk and causes you body image distress. Now, I'll explain exactly what this "something" is and I'll tell you what you can do about it.

SILENT ASSUMPTIONS ABOUT YOUR APPEARANCE

Whether due to traumatic insults ("Hey, Elephant Girl" or "Look at Bony Boy"), family messages ("Look how pretty your sister is" or "Your complexion looks terrible" or "You're pudgy and need to go on a diet"), or cultural socialization ("Thin is in and feminine" and "Real men have massive muscles"), you've learned certain basic beliefs or assumptions about the meaning of your looks in your life. These core assumptions, which psychologists call *schemas*, determine how you interpret reality. They operate like templates or guides that influence what you pay attention to, how you think about the events in your life, and how you think about yourself. Your schemas are so much a part of you that you've ceased being aware of them; they are "self-evident truths" that you mindlessly take for granted.

Like everyone, you have various schemas that guide your thoughts about all kinds of things, such as love and relationships, success and failure, and the meaning of gender or race. You also have assumptions that direct how you think about your own physical characteristics. I call these self-schemas *Appearance Assumptions*. Appearance Assumptions are your core beliefs about the relevance and influence of your looks in your life. They concern the extent to which you define yourself and your self-worth on the basis of what you look like. You probably never stop to question their accuracy. Most likely, you ignore or reject any possible evidence that your Appearance Assumptions might be off base. Appearance Assumptions are your body image "rulers"—in both senses of this word. They are the dictators of your Private Body Talk, and they are the yardsticks by which you measure your physical acceptability.

Take a look at the following diagram (figure 4.1). It shows how Appearance Assumptions eventually lead to the emotions you feel that relate to your appearance.

Figure 4.1
From Assumptions to Emotions

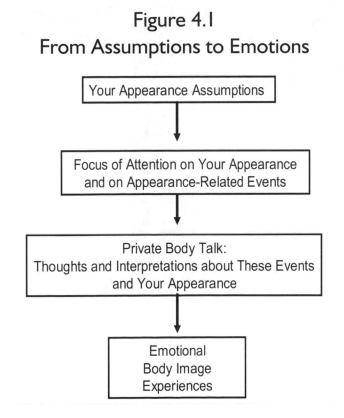

In Step 1 of the workbook, one of the self-tests you took, the Appearance Importance Test, provided an index of your Appearance Assumptions—your investment in your looks for self-worth. Go back to your Body Image Profile and see what your results were for this self-test. If you scored in the Risky or Problem Zones, then Step 4 has plenty of help to offer you.

HOW APPEARANCE ASSUMPTIONS DICTATE YOUR DISCONTENT

My computer stores research data from hundreds of people who answered the same body image self-tests that you took in Step 1. I divided these people into two groups. The first group are "Assumers"—those who agreed with most Appearance Assumptions from the Appearance Importance Test. The second group, "Doubters," disagreed with most assumptions. I compared Assumers and Doubters to find out what percentage of each group revealed body image difficulties on the three of the other self-tests. The results in figure 4.2 are quite striking. Here's what they reveal.

Figure 4.2
How Do Appearance Assumptions Affect Your Body Image?

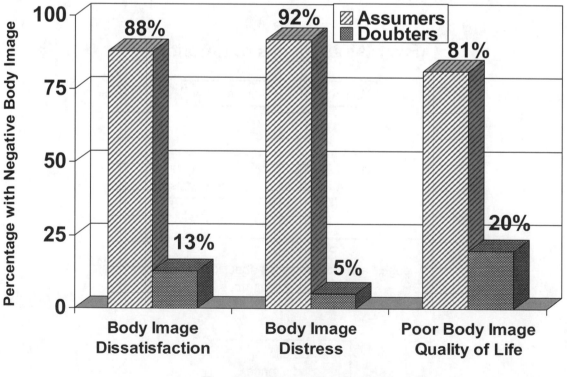

On each self-test, the vast majority of Assumers clearly had more problematic body image experiences than the Doubters did. They were much more dissatisfied with most aspects of their appearance. They more often felt body image distress across a range of everyday situations. They experienced a much poorer body image quality of life, with more adverse consequences to their social and psychological well-being. Appearance Assumption Doubters seldom had a negative body image. They had a more positive, accepting view of their appearance, had episodes of body image distress infrequently, and felt that their body image contributed favorably to the quality of their lives.

Assumers' Private Body Talk always seems to disrupt their peace of mind, while Doubters are more clearheaded about their looks. Step 4 will enable you become a Doubter instead of an Assumer.

TEN TAXING APPEARANCE ASSUMPTIONS

There are numerous Appearance Assumptions that can influence your body image experiences. However, let's focus on ten particularly potent beliefs. These are listed in the Self-Discovery Helpsheet below. Before reading any further, please complete this Helpsheet.

Self-Discovery Helpsheet: Ten Appearance Assumptions

Read each statement below and check those that you honestly believe to be true or mostly true.

☐   1. Physically attractive people have it all.

☐   2. My worth as a person depends on how I look.

☐   3. I should always do whatever I can to look my best.

☐   4. The first thing that people will notice about me is what's wrong with my appearance.

☐   5. If people knew how I really look, they would probably like me less.

☐   6. By managing my physical appearance, I can control my social and emotional life.

☐   7. My appearance is responsible for much of what has happened to me in my life.

☐   8. If I could look just as I wish, my life would be much happier.

☐   9. My culture's messages make it impossible for me to be satisfied with my appearance.

☐   10. The only way I could ever accept my looks would be to change my looks.

Conversing with Your Assumptions: Your New Inner Voice

Self-esteem comes from the ability to experience yourself honestly and accurately. There are two psychological forces that may lead you to play mind games in which you hold a distorted view of yourself and your body image. These forces prevent you from making worthwhile changes. The first is *self-deception*. Because honest self-awareness can make you uncomfortable with your shortcomings, you may deceive yourself to achieve a false sense of self-acceptance. For example, you may gloss over or deny how demeaning your Private Body Talk is because you'd prefer not to think of yourself as so viciously self-critical.

A second force that may lead you to play mind games is based on a *need for self-consistency*. You've decided that your view of yourself is the absolute truth, so you can see only things that consistently confirm these self-perceptions, however unflattering. For example, you may have convinced yourself that your nasty inner conversations about your looks are the only valid view that could possibly exist. You insist that you should have a negative body image. If this is so, then, obviously, your self-deception and your need for self-consistency will interfere with your being able to change what you need to change to be happier with your appearance and yourself.

Cognitive therapy can help you develop honest and accepting self-awareness. This approach teaches you how to find, listen to, and nurture that aspect of yourself that I call your New Inner Voice. This voice speaks in ways that are mindful, understanding, tolerant, fair, realistic, logical, and assured. This New Inner Voice doesn't care where you are on anybody's scale of physical attractiveness. It cares about and accepts you! It doesn't sound a bit like the old critical voice of your upsetting Private Body Talk.

Impeaching your long-standing Appearance Assumptions isn't easy. The first words of your New Inner Voice will simply question the validity and value of your assumptions, purposefully challenging their authority over your thoughts and emotions. Each assumption paints a picture, and your New Inner Voice will ask, "What's wrong with this picture?" Each is an arguable assumption, containing a bit of truth and a lot of falsehood. Tackling the ten Appearance Assumptions, one at a time, will make you more aware of the falsehoods and leave you with a more reasonable mind-set. After reading about these assumptions, you will use a Helpsheet for Change to create a New Inner Voice that speaks to each assumption.

Assumption 1: Physically Attractive People Have It All

Society's preoccupation with and marketing of physical attractiveness reinforces the assumption that being good-looking pays bigger benefits than it actually does. The undeniable truth is that being good-looking is sometimes advantageous. However, as the French author Stendhal asserted in his famous essay on love in 1822, "Beauty is only the promise of happiness." Nonetheless, for many reasons, attractiveness doesn't keep most of its promises. There are also plenty of reasons why being average-looking or less doesn't close off opportunities for happiness. To help you challenge Appearance Assumption 1, I want to take a few pages here to explain to you why looks aren't everything. These are not reasons that I made up; these are facts established by scientific research on the psychology of physical appearance (Cash 1990; Feingold 1992; Jackson 1992).

- Fact 1: *Beauty is as beauty does.* It's true. Actions do speak more loudly than looks. Friendliness, warmth, intelligence, honesty, a sense of humor, and social sensitivity are highly valued human traits, regardless of what you look like. Think about people who are important in your life. Are they all perfect 10s on the appearance scale? I'll bet their looks aren't that crucial to how you feel about them.

- Fact 2: *First impressions don't always last.* Our initial reactions to someone's appearance are not frozen forever in our minds. We come to see good people as increasingly good-looking. Have you ever met a person whose appearance wasn't so appealing, but as your relationship evolved, that person's looks seemed more and more interesting and attractive? On the other hand, have you ever noticed how the halo of physical attractiveness can fade over time? In 1903, playwright George Bernard Shaw aptly observed, "Beauty is all very well at first sight, but who ever looks at it when it has been in the house three days?"

- Fact 3: *Birds of a feather do flock together.* We are often attracted to people who are similar to us in certain ways. For example, we seek out those with shared interests, ethnic heritage, religious or political values, and educational background. This is sometimes true of physical appearance as well. Many times, best friends, dates, and mates are comparable in physical attractiveness. This pairing off based on similarity of attractiveness has the fortunate result that nobody gets left out.

- Fact 4: *Beauty can backfire by implying egotism.* Appearance Assumption 1 ignores the "ugly faces of beauty." Paradoxically, the assumed advantages of physical attractiveness can cause disadvantages. If we believe that good-looking people are desirable and reap social benefits, we may also think that they are well aware of their good looks and their privileged status. So we infer that they must be self-absorbed and opportunistic. Then, we may assume they are less responsible or trustworthy as friends, romantic partners, or parents. This negative (and false) stereotype of attractive people can complicate or cancel the benefits of their looks.

- Fact 5: *Beauty can backfire because of sexism.* Another factor that undermines the power of attractiveness is sexism. Pretty women are sometimes presumed to possess "feminine" personality traits, such as passivity and emotionality. Handsome guys are sometimes thought to have "masculine" characteristics, such as a dominant personality and a low "emotional IQ." Although these stereotypes are untrue, such sexist biases about physical attractiveness erode some of its positive power.

- Fact 6: *Beauty breeds envy and jealousy.* The eighteenth-century historian Edward Gibbon once said that "beauty is an outward gift which is seldom despised, except by those to whom it has been refused." Have you ever heard anyone exclaim, "They are so good-looking (or thin, or well built). I hate them"? When we compare ourselves to people who have the looks we idealize, we usually end up feeling worse about our own appearance and then we dislike these good-looking people for "making" us feel unattractive. My own research has concluded that people who are highly invested in being physically attractive are more likely to distrust and disparage good-looking people of their own sex.

- Fact 7: *Beauty can transform people into sex objects.* In a well-known popular song, Rod Stewart posed the question "Do ya think I'm sexy?" Although most of us want our romantic partners to find us sexy, few of us enjoy being seen solely as a sex object by everyone we encounter. Good-looking people, especially women, are often subjected to unwelcome sexual comments about their bodies. These remarks are frequently demeaning and harassing. Would you really want to be seen as only a sexy body or a pretty face?

- Fact 8: *Beauty can foster self-doubt.* Fact 7, above, gives rise to another problem for attractive people: They may think that people are nice to them only because they are attractive. Allow me to explain this by repeating a conversation I once had with my longtime friend, Nancy, who is strikingly lovely. One day, I complimented her, telling her how beautiful I thought she was. To my surprise, she became very upset and said, "I thought you liked me for who I am. Now, I'll never be sure that it's not just because of what I happen to look like." Nancy's point poses important questions. Wouldn't you rather know that people like you because you're a splendid person and not merely because you're nice to look at? Wouldn't you rather feel that you deserve the recognition you get than have to wonder if somebody's being nice to you just because he or she is enchanted with your looks?

- Fact 9: *Beauty is a weak foundation for self-esteem.* The more people invest in a "beauty bank," the more vulnerable their self-worth becomes. So, contrary to Appearance Assumption 1, good-looking people don't have it all, if "it all" rests on being attractive. Time and life events alter one's appearance—for better or worse. A foundation for self-worth built on beauty is a shaky foundation indeed.

- Fact 10: *Looks don't matter to everybody.* The nineteenth-century poet Robert Southey wrote, "How little do they see what is, who frame their hasty judgments upon that which seems." We all know "nearsighted" people who judge others solely on appearances. Fortunately, however, there are many people who aren't swayed by whether we're fat or skinny, "dressed to the nines" or wearing our comfy but "sloppy" clothes. They don't expect us to look perfect. They see us and appreciate us for who we are. We should all try to become more like these terrific appearance-blind individuals. They make our world a more just and accepting place.

Changing a negative body image requires that you seriously question Assumption 1 and keep your looks in perspective. Your New Inner Voice will remind you that beauty is a mixed bag that contains many false promises. In the absence of a positive body image and solid self-esteem, good looks aren't worth much. Relinquishing stereotypes and pursuits of physical perfection will free you to embrace many opportunities for appreciating yourself.

Assumption 2: My Worth as a Person Depends on How I Look

This important assumption is really at the root of the body image problems of many people. It asserts that your physical appearance is the only or the most crucial aspect of everything that you are. You believe that you are defined by your looks more than by all the assets of your personality, your actions, or your experiences. This belief can lead you to minimize your many fine qualities that have nothing to do with your looks. It can lead you to spend huge amounts of time thinking about or worrying about what you see when you look in the mirror, as well as countless hours trying to create or enhance the looks that you deem essential to your self-worth or social worth. This is a dictatorial assumption that you must challenge! How?

- Mindfully take inventory of all the other aspects of yourself that represent who you are. What are the qualities you possess that you really are happy about? What are your attributes that people who know you value? For example, are you funny? Are you kind, considerate, and emotionally open to others? Are you a good listener? Are you quite knowledgeable about certain topics? What do you like about yourself?

- You need to start hearing your New Inner Voice say, "Instead of what I look like, it's really my caring attitude, infectious sense of humor, devotion to family, competence at my job, conversational skills, ethics and morality, dependability, and so on, that reflect my special worth." In other words, you need to begin to recognize that your looks are less important in defining you than many other attributes of yours.

Assumption 3: I Should Always Do Whatever I Can to Look My Best

The words "should" and "always" imply that looking your best is your duty and that by not looking your best you have failed. Ask yourself the following questions about this assumption:

First of all, why have you saddled yourself with this obligation? What do you expect will happen if you can look your best on all occasions? What might happen if you can't? Looking your best is extremely subjective, so how will you know you've performed your duty? Who can possibly look his or her best all the time? Because we can always imagine ways we might look better, this assumption sets you up for failure by requiring the impossible. Do you require other people to have the best imaginable appearance at all times? Would you be so harshly judgmental if a friend wore less than perfectly flattering clothing, had a hair out of place, or got a zit? I hope not. Nor do I hope that you would tolerate such a demanding expectation from a friend. So why should you demand this of yourself? It's nice to feel that you look nice; it's not nice to feel that you *always* have to.

Your New Inner Voice will speak out against perfectionism: "I enjoy liking how I look, but I could loosen up some. I don't have to look perfect all the time. When I look less than my best, nobody ever commands me to look better—nobody but me! I'm the one pressuring myself. I'm the one giving myself grief! I need to do whatever I can to accept my looks. It's okay to look acceptable, rather than look exceptional."

Assumption 4: The First Thing That People Will Notice About Me Is What's Wrong with My Appearance

Again, this is only a partial truth. Heads will turn if you have spiked orange hair, a large pierced nose ring, or a likeness of Bugs Bunny tattooed on your forehead. But then, you probably want others to take notice. What about having physical characteristics that are not of your choosing? Here's what you must realize in questioning Assumption 4:

- If you're obese or have a pronounced physical disfigurement, few folks will fail to notice. That's the reality of human nature. We all notice what people look like. But, so what? Just because others are aware of this doesn't mean that they'll despise or mistreat you, or that your life is ruined. Your own actions are up to you. Your personality—your friendliness, good humor, kindness, conversational skills, and so forth—is much more influential than whatever might be "wrong" with your looks.

- Assumption 4 is false about most people most of the time. What is true is that you are the one observing what you don't like about your appearance. Other people usually couldn't care less. They've got other things to think about. Of course, if they, too, have a negative body image, they're probably busy being self-conscious and worrying that you will notice their physical imperfections.

- Your New Inner Voice will help you keep things in perspective. It will be saying, "So what if people notice that I'm short, or heavy, or balding, or have a facial scar, or whatever? What difference does that really make? Life goes on! I'm a pretty likable person. People tell me they like me because I'm …."

Assumption 5: If People Knew How I Really Look, They Would Probably Like Me Less

Assumption 5 is akin to Assumption 4, as both reflect your belief that people are judgmental about your looks. For Assumption 5, however, you believe that others would judge you harshly "if they only knew." This assumption breeds shame. Believing it will force you into hiding—to conceal those aspects of your physical self that you think other people find repulsive. You worry about what you assume to be the hidden or "naked truth." The problem with this assumption is that it becomes an untested truth. Disproving Assumption 5 requires that you test it. Hiding only makes you feel worse.

A client of mine, a college student named Harriet, did this program. She had always been ashamed of her "thick legs" and was convinced that anyone who saw them would stare at them in disgust. So she always wore long pants. Finally, one hot day when the program was ending, she conjured up the courage to bring her legs out of hiding and wear shorts to school. She saw me walking across the campus and approached me. "Look, I'm wearing shorts!" Harriet exclaimed. "So far, nobody's run away in horror. I can't believe I avoided doing this for so long."

- Try this indirect test: Ask yourself how often you stopped liking someone upon discovering some imperfection in his or her appearance. How often have you said or thought something like "I didn't know that Matthew has an appendectomy scar. I'll be sure to avoid him from now on"? Or, "Now that I've seen Sharon without her makeup on, I have no more use for her"? Or, "Becky's breasts are smaller than I first thought they were, so that's the end of our relationship"?

- In Step 6, I'll help you come out of hiding and test this assumption directly, as Harriet did. Once we test the assumption, we typically find that we have been mistaken all along. People accept us, flaws and all. And that feels so much better, and so much more real, than hiding. Your New Inner Voice will help you keep matters in perspective. You are the one who is uncomfortable with your physical feature. It's your own shame, not somebody else's judgment. If people knew how you really look, their opinions would not, in fact, change. Everyone else would be more accepting of you than you are.

- Your New Inner Voice will coax you out of hiding. Listen to it. It will say something like "I worried that I'd be rejected and hurt if people knew how I really look … that if they saw what I don't like about my body, they'd be revolted and I'd feel bad. But all my worrying makes me feel bad. Would I really feel that much worse if I stopped concealing what I look like? Is it possible that I'm making this into a bigger issue than it really is?"

Assumption 6: By Managing My Physical Appearance, I Can Control My Social and Emotional Life

You have tremendous control over your looks. Consider all the available tools for managing your appearance—clothing, cosmetics, jewelry, hairstyling, hair-coloring, a healthy diet, regular exercise, and sensible skin care. Good grooming can certainly enhance your looks and make you feel attractive. The hazard, however, comes from relying excessively on these tools and believing that they are necessities instead of niceties.

- In arguing with Assumption 6, you must start to see that you cannot effectively manage your self-esteem and your life by asking your appearance to do all the work. Just as a carpenter cannot construct a house with only a hammer, you cannot build a happy life using only your looks.

- Appearance management works only if it improves your body image. Stylish clothes are useless if you don't like how you look in them. Moreover, as you saw for Assumption 5, if all the clothes do is cover parts of your body that you dislike, they aren't really helping your body image. Depending on clothing for damage control only reinforces your belief that your unadorned body is objectionable.

- Review your own experiences for evidence that contradicts Assumption 6. If all your appearance-managing efforts to control your social and emotional life are so effective, then why do you still have a negative body image? We can reword Assumption 6 and make it truer; for example, "By changing my body image, I can better control my social and emotional life."

- What will your New Inner Voice say to help you modify this faulty assumption? It will say, "Spending too much effort trying to 'fix' my looks is misdirected effort. Constant repairs on my appearance are only a temporary Band-Aid. I'm still unhappy with my looks. I want to feel better permanently. So, I need to focus on changing my mind instead of my looks. That's a change that will give me more control over my life."

Assumption 7: My Appearance Is Responsible for Much of What Has Happened to Me in My Life

Yes, your appearance has affected some things in your life. At times it paid off, and at times it was a detriment. Nevertheless, most things that have happened in your life had absolutely nothing to do with your looks. Most were either the product of your personality, intelligence, decisions, and actions, or were simply the result of chance or another person's actions.

- History demonstrates that attractiveness is not a prerequisite for success in most endeavors of life other than certain media, performance, or modeling roles. Abraham Lincoln, Winston Churchill, Mikhail Gorbachev, Henry Kissinger, and former New York mayors Ed Koch and Rudy Giuliani wouldn't exactly qualify as handsome hunks. Golda Meir, Eleanor Roosevelt, Margaret Thatcher, and Mother Teresa would be unlikely winners of a beauty contest. What widely respected leaders from world history, the arts, or literature can you think of who were not, in your opinion, good-looking? Of course, if you choose your heroes or heroines only from movies or other parts of the media culture based on their physical attractiveness, you are not selecting fairly. Most people we've personally known who have meaningfully touched our lives aren't necessarily great-looking. Can you think of individuals whom you have loved or admired for reasons that had nothing to do with their looks? This is not a rhetorical question. I really want you to think about it.

- Your New Inner Voice argues against Assumption 7 by realizing and saying, "My appearance may have influenced some things in my life, but ultimately, I'm responsible for my life. I can make choices about how I deal with any effects that my looks have. Though my history has already been written, my present and my future are up to me, not to my appearance."

Assumption 8: If I Could Look Just as I Wish, My Life Would Be Much Happier

The trouble with Assumption 8 is its implication: Unless I can look the way I want to (that is, taller, thinner, more muscular, less wrinkled, or with a straighter nose), there's no way I can be happy. What makes you unhappy is not your physical appearance. It's your wish that sells you short and robs you of self-acceptance. Challenge this assumption in these ways:

- Remember this scientifically established truth: Physically attractive people are not necessarily happier than less attractive people. Good-looking individuals have their body image wish lists too.

- Have you ever had experiences in which the more desperately you wanted something, the less you appreciated what you had? To justify your wishing for "the new" you have to berate "the old." Your burning desires destroy your ability to enjoy what you have. Wishing magnifies your discontent, which you believe can be resolved only by getting what you wish.

- Your New Inner Voice can put you in touch with reality. It reminds you that your goal is to achieve a better body image, not to have a different body. Listen to your New Inner Voice say, "I realize that my appearance doesn't really prevent me from being happy. I do know this: I make myself unhappy trying to look like my idealized image. I cause myself despair by beating myself up for my wishes not coming true. Once I learn to accept my looks, my life will be much happier. That's up to me, not my body."

Assumption 9: My Culture's Messages Make It Impossible for Me to Be Satisfied with My Appearance

With this assumption, you make yourself into a victim. Poor me! So you've come to feel powerless? Then, what's the use in trying to change your negative body image? Okay, it's certainly true that the cultural media convey powerful and unhelpful images and messages about physical appearance. They try to convince you there are only two ways that you can be happy and succeed in life. Either you must be born with good looks or you must buy all the products and services needed to manufacture physical perfection. Let's take a closer look at Assumption 9:

- Genius isn't required to recognize how extreme and distorted these messages are. If they were all-controlling, no one would have a positive body image. And some people do like their looks despite these unhelpful forces. That's because they know that personal fulfillment does not require physical perfection. Do you know what is certain to be much worse than not being a perfect 10? It's worrying about not being a perfect 10.

- The media and the huge "appearance industry" certainly make it difficult to accept your body, but difficult isn't the same as impossible. They are indeed a brainwashing force to be reckoned with, but they are not aiming a loaded gun at you and commanding you to "believe and do everything we say, or else!" What you believe and what you do is entirely up to you. Think about it.

- So what do you do? A character in the movie *Network* proclaimed the media's injustices by yelling from a rooftop to the passive public below, "I'm mad as hell, and I'm not gonna take it anymore!" You don't have to take it anymore either. Should you trash your television and cease reading magazines or watching music videos? Should you boycott all appearance-altering products and services? Probably not. Our society could certainly use improvements, but the best place to start is within yourself. Your own Private Body Talk does not have to echo the media's appearance-preoccupied voices. You don't have to be a victim. Body-accepting individuals have learned how to see these cultural messages as distorted and irrelevant and to tune them out.

- Your New Inner Voice will be assertive and will empower you not to take it anymore. It will say, "I'm tired of expecting myself to look like all these perfect bodies in the media. Seeing them isn't believing them. I'm not them and I don't have to look like them. I'm going to work hard to accept myself. The media don't make it impossible for me to accept my looks. I do."

Assumption 10: The Only Way I Could Ever Accept My Looks Would Be to Change My Looks

This is one very self-defeating assumption! It drives people to try just about anything to alter or "correct" their appearance. My new clients often want me to help them lose weight or refer them to a cosmetic surgeon. They believe that only then would they have a positive body image. When I suggest that we should first work on body image and then decide about weight loss or surgery, they look at me with disappointment and disbelief. They think I don't I understand what they need so that they can be happy.

- I understand the basis and power of Appearance Assumption 10. If something is broken, fix it. So, you go on a diet again, work out a lot, buy new clothes, get a different hair-style, use the expensive wrinkle product, or have cosmetic surgery. Maybe you've done some of these things, and some even felt pretty good—for a while. But if all the fixes still haven't repaired how you feel about your looks, ask yourself the obvious question: "What's really broken?" What's not working here is your body image, and that's what needs fixing.

- Research I described earlier in this workbook confirms that you can improve your body image without altering your body. Here's the corrected version of Assumption 10: "The only way I could ever like my looks would be to change my body image."

- Tackle Assumption 10 head on! Your New Inner Voice urges you to shift your emphasis: Say to yourself, "I've spent too much of my life trying to change my looks. What I need to do is focus on the real problem and real solutions. Fixing my appearance feels good at the moment, but it doesn't last. I just keep looking for more ways to be better-looking. The best way that I can like my body is to work directly on my body image. That's really the problem I need to fix."

YOUR NEW INNER VOICE SPEAKS OUT

Establishing reasonable doubt of faulty Appearance Assumptions requires more than a casual commitment to stop thinking those things. Change comes only from actively doing something to create a new attitude. A New Inner Voice will create a new attitude. This strong voice will speak realistically about appearance, in language that enables you to take responsibility for how you think and feel, no matter what you look like. It is a voice of tolerance and reason. A New Inner Voice will understand that your body image affects the quality of your life more than your body's actual appearance does.

Cultivating your own New Inner Voice is crucial to developing a more favorable body image. It's okay that right now this voice may be only a whisper in your mind. You can give it the words it needs to speak more clearly and forcefully. And then you can listen to it and hear it. Here's how: The following ten Helpsheets for Change: Arguing with My Appearance Assumptions, will help you to develop and nurture your New Inner Voice. Use your own words to talk to yourself about each arguable assumption listed. Read over the arguments against each assumption that I've discussed above. Think hard about other possible arguments. Don't expect to believe everything you write. Write down what you want to believe—what sounds healthier, more rational, and more accepting of yourself.

On the Helpsheet for each Appearance Assumption, begin by (1) noting how the assumption influences what you pay attention to, (2) what automatic thoughts run though your mind, and then (3) how you feel. Finally (4) write out your arguments against each Appearance Assumption, even those you didn't check earlier in your Self-Discovery Helpsheet as statements you find true or mostly true. After putting your words into writing, read them out loud to yourself.

Next, try to find ways to express your New Inner Voice to other people, including those who know about and support your efforts to develop a more positive body image. If we convey these new, desired beliefs to others, the beliefs are more likely to become our own. At first, your New Inner Voice may seem foreign to you—like somebody else talking. That's okay; that's understandable. Each day, take a few minutes to reread your words aloud. Soon this voice will begin to sound familiar and the wisdom of your New Inner Voice will become self-evident.

Helpsheet for Change: Arguing with My Appearance Assumptions

1. When I assume that "physically attractive people have it all,"

Then I focus on:

_____

_____

_____

And I think:

_____

_____

_____

And I feel:

_____

_____

_____

My New Inner Voice argues with this Appearance Assumption:

_____

_____

_____

_____

_____

_____

_____

_____

_____

_____

_____

Helpsheet for Change: Arguing with My Appearance Assumptions

2. When I assume that "my worth as a person depends on how I look,"

Then I focus on:

_____

_____

_____

And I think:

_____

_____

_____

And I feel:

_____

_____

_____

My New Inner Voice argues with this Appearance Assumption:

_____

_____

_____

_____

_____

_____

_____

_____

_____

_____

Helpsheet for Change: Arguing with My Appearance Assumptions

3. When I assume that "I should always do whatever I can to look my best,"

Then I focus on:

_____

_____

_____

And I think:

_____

_____

_____

And I feel:

_____

_____

_____

My New Inner Voice argues with this Appearance Assumption:

_____

_____

_____

_____

_____

_____

_____

_____

Helpsheet for Change: Arguing with My Appearance Assumptions

4. When I assume that "the first thing that people will notice about me is what's wrong with my appearance,"

Then I focus on:

_____

_____

_____

And I think:

_____

_____

_____

And I feel:

_____

_____

_____

My New Inner Voice argues with this Appearance Assumption:

_____

_____

_____

_____

_____

_____

_____

_____

Helpsheet for Change: Arguing with My Appearance Assumptions

5. When I assume that "if people knew how I really look, they would probably like me less,"

Then I focus on:

_____

_____

_____

And I think:

_____

_____

_____

And I feel:

_____

_____

_____

My New Inner Voice argues with this Appearance Assumption:

_____

_____

_____

_____

_____

_____

_____

_____

Helpsheet for Change: Arguing with My Appearance Assumptions

6. When I assume that "by managing my physical appearance, I can control my
   social and emotional life,"

Then I focus on:

_____

_____

_____

And I think:

_____

_____

_____

And I feel:

_____

_____

_____

My New Inner Voice argues with this Appearance Assumption:

_____

_____

_____

_____

_____

_____

_____

_____

Helpsheet for Change: Arguing with My Appearance Assumptions

7. When I assume that "my appearance is responsible for much of what has happened to me in my life,"

Then I focus on:

_____

_____

_____

And I think:

_____

_____

_____

And I feel:

_____

_____

_____

My New Inner Voice argues with this Appearance Assumption:

_____

_____

_____

_____

_____

_____

_____

_____

Helpsheet for Change: Arguing with My Appearance Assumptions

8. When I assume that "if I could look as I wish, my life would be much happier,"

Then I focus on:

_____

_____

_____

And I think:

_____

_____

_____

And I feel:

_____

_____

_____

My New Inner Voice argues with this Appearance Assumption:

_____

_____

_____

_____

_____

_____

_____

_____

_____

_____

Helpsheet for Change: Arguing with My Appearance Assumptions

9. When I assume that "my culture's messages make it impossible for me to be satisfied with my appearance,"

Then I focus on:

_____

_____

_____

And I think:

_____

_____

_____

And I feel:

_____

_____

_____

My New Inner Voice argues with this Appearance Assumption:

_____

_____

_____

_____

_____

_____

_____

_____

_____

Helpsheet for Change: Arguing with My Appearance Assumptions

10. When I assume that "the only way I could ever accept my looks would be to change my looks,"

Then I focus on:

_____

_____

_____

And I think:

_____

_____

_____

And I feel:

_____

_____

_____

My New Inner Voice argues with this Appearance Assumption:

_____

_____

_____

_____

_____

_____

_____

_____

_____

FINAL WORDS OF ENCOURAGEMENT

A lot of people decide to change something in their lives—something they know they really need to change. Maybe it's their job, or a relationship, or where they live, or a bad habit. They've even told their friends or loved ones that they need to make a change. They know they want to be happier, and they see the direction they need to take. They start on a new path, taking the right steps. They're actually getting there. At about this point in the road, they wish they had already reached their destination. "Are we there yet?"

Impatience during a transition from a bad place to a good place is a normal human reaction. We've all felt this way. It just means that we really want to be in a better place, and that's good. Just be mindful of your experiences of impatience. You need not judge yourself or this program because of this feeling. Accept that your progress may not be as rapid as you'd wish it to be. Use your impatience to be where you want to be. Step 5 is coming up and it will offer even more opportunities to strengthen your New Inner Voice. When you reach the end of this workbook you'll be fluent in this new language. And you will have reached your destination.

Mindfully Modifying Your Mental Mistakes

Camille is not only convinced that she's physically unattractive, she's also convinced her looks are wrecking her life. She is certain that everyone she knows thinks she's ugly and that, unless she can do something to fix her physical flaws, she's doomed to a life of rejection and unhappiness. She blames her looks for all of her past problems.

Camille spends a considerable amount of her mental energy comparing herself with other women who look the way she wishes she could look. She often talks herself out of doing fun things because she expects she will be self-conscious about her appearance and for that reason unable to enjoy herself. Whenever she's stressed about work or social concerns, her body image worsens.

If you were to look at Camille, you might notice that she has some freckles, and if you looked very closely, you might see that her nose isn't perfectly straight. You might also guess that she is slightly overweight. But you wouldn't really care about these characteristics, because they are just an incidental part of who she is. To Camille, on the other hand, they are practically everything.

Do you, like Camille, disturb your mind and life with your negative view of your own looks? Long ago, in the first century AD, the philosopher Epictetus wisely asserted, "What disturbs people's minds is not events but their judgments on events." The essence of his wisdom is that our emotions depend upon our point of view as we try to make sense of our experiences.

In Step 4, you learned how your Appearance Assumptions lay out the basic road maps for your Private Body Talk. Your thoughts about your looks then travel these well-worn paths. Your Appearance Assumptions are joined by another force that directs your Private Body Talk—*Cognitive Distortions*. These are specific mental mistakes that steer your inner conversations along crooked paths that send you in the wrong direction and down dead ends where it's difficult to turn around. Appearance Assumptions set the stage for the general focus of your attention and thoughts in relation to your looks. Cognitive Distortions are the specific mental manifestations or contents of your thoughts. Appearance Assumptions pave the way for faulty, error-prone Private Body Talk, and your Cognitive Distortions manufacture the mental mistakes.

DISCOVERING YOUR BODY IMAGE DISTORTIONS

Cognitive therapists teach their clients how to recognize and eradicate mental mistakes from their inner conversations. Step 5 teaches you how to become your own cognitive therapist. This Step will enable you to develop a more reasonable, rational, and accepting Private Body Talk. As a result, negative feelings about your appearance will be less likely to occur and less disruptive to your daily life.

As a clinician and a researcher, I've found that people with a negative body image tend to make the same mental mistakes. The following Self-Discovery Helpsheet contains a self-test that will enable you to learn about your own patterns of thought. First, complete this Helpsheet, being totally mindful and honest about how you typically think. Afterward, I'll define the eight common Body Image Distortions for you and teach you how to address these in your own body image experiences.

Self-Discovery Helpsheet: Thinking About Your Thinking

This questionnaire asks you to become aware of your own mental conversations, especially mental conversations about your physical appearance. Each question below presents a hypothetical situation and a mental conversation that some people might have in that situation. Please imagine yourself in each situation. Read the thought pattern that is described. Then decide how characteristic that thought pattern would be of your mental conversations.

	Mostly Like Me	Mostly *Not* Like Me
1. Imagine that you weighed a few more pounds than your ideal weight. Would you think, "Until I lose these few pounds, I look really fat"?	☐	☐
2. Imagine that on a particular day, you develop a few acne zits on your face. Would you think, "These zits make me look ugly"?	☐	☐
3. Imagine that on a certain day your hair doesn't look "right." Would you think, "I look awful today"?	☐	☐
4. Imagine that you leave for work or school one morning feeling that you don't look quite as good as you usually do. Would you think, "I really look terrible today"?	☐	☐
5. Imagine you see yourself and a group of friends and acquaintances in a photograph. Would you compare yourself with whomever looks best in the picture?	☐	☐

	Mostly Like Me	Mostly Not Like Me
6. Imagine that you're trying on new swimsuits you've seen in newspaper ads. Would you think, "This suit doesn't look nearly as good on me as it does on the model in the ad"?	☐	☐
7. Imagine that you're watching TV and on the commercials there are attractive people of your gender. Would you compare your looks to theirs and then think that you really don't look very good?	☐	☐
8. Imagine that you go to the gym or to the beach or pool. There are some "perfect bodies" there. Would you compare your body to theirs and think that these people make you look bad?	☐	☐
9. Imagine that you're with friends who are discussing what certain other friends look like. Would you privately begin to think about what's "wrong" with your physical appearance?	☐	☐
10. Imagine that you're getting ready to go out and you're looking at your appearance in the mirror. Would you ignore looking at or thinking about your best features?	☐	☐
11. Imagine someone comments favorably on your appearance. Would you then have thoughts about aspects of your appearance that you think would never be complimented?	☐	☐
12. Imagine that you're looking at your nude body in the mirror. Would you focus on your "flaws" more than you would your physical assets?	☐	☐
13. Imagine that you're single and go out on a blind date. You both seem to have a pretty good time. Your date says, "I'll call you in a couple of days," but never does. Would you think, "My looks probably messed things up"?	☐	☐
14. Imagine that you're out with people you don't know very well. You notice that some of these people are very friendly with others but not with you. Would you think that the reason they weren't attentive to you had something to do with your appearance?	☐	☐
15. Imagine that you're single, go to a party, and meet someone you find attractive. This person leaves with another nice-looking person at the end of the night. Would you think, "My looks probably weren't good enough"?	☐	☐
16. You are thinking about some of the disappointments in your life. Would you wonder if things would have turned out better if you had looked different?	☐	☐
17. When you think about the aspects of your appearance with which you're dissatisfied, do you think that most people also dislike those aspects of your looks?	☐	☐

	Mostly Like Me	Mostly Not Like Me
18. Imagine that you're exercising in an aerobics class. Would you be convinced that those people who are watching you are doing so because they're noticing some flaw in your body as you exercise?	☐	☐
19. Imagine that you're wearing a new outfit and no one comments on it. Would you assume that people think the outfit doesn't look good on you?	☐	☐
20. Imagine that your lover shows little interest in making love with you for a few weeks. Would you think that the reason is that your partner thinks you're physically unappealing in some way?	☐	☐
21. Think about those aspects of your appearance that you've wished were different. Do you ever think that your future will be less satisfying because of how you look?	☐	☐
22. Imagine that you're single and down on your luck with dating. Would you think, "As I long as I look as I do, nobody will ever fall in love with me"?	☐	☐
23. Imagine that you've moved to a different area and are interested in meeting new friends. Would you have thoughts that your physical appearance could lead people to reject you as a possible friend?	☐	☐
24. Imagine that you're invited to a party on the beach. Would you think that because of something about your appearance you probably won't fit in or enjoy participating?	☐	☐
25. Imagine that you're shopping for some new clothes. Do you talk yourself out of trying certain attractive styles or colors because they might call attention to parts of your body you don't like?	☐	☐
26. Imagine that you're single and are dating someone you really like. Would you think that there are some "undesirable" parts of your body that you should hide from your partner?	☐	☐
27. Imagine that you want to work out at the gym. Would you think that you need to look more fit before you can go to the gym to work out in front of others?	☐	☐
28. Imagine that some neighbors drop by unexpectedly and you have not yet worked on your appearance for the day. Would you think, "I can't answer the door and let them see me like this"?	☐	☐
29. Imagine that you're stressed out one day. Would you be more likely to have negative thoughts about your looks?	☐	☐

	Mostly Like Me	Mostly *Not* Like Me
30. Imagine you feel that something is not quite right about your looks, and you ask a friend for feedback. Your friend reassures you that you look fine. Would you dismiss the reassurances because you know that how you feel must be the real truth?	☐	☐
31. Imagine that you had a large meal and feel overly full. Would feeling full make you think that you're fat?	☐	☐
32. Imagine that you have a new haircut and aren't particularly happy about how it looks. Would you then have critical thoughts about other aspects of your appearance, as well?	☐	☐

For each type of distortion, how many items (from 0 to 4) did you endorse in the Mostly Like Me column?

Beauty-or-Beast Distortion (items 1-4) _____

Unfair-to-Compare Distortion (items 5-8) _____

The Magnifying Glass Distortion (items 9-12) _____

The Blame Game Distortion (items 13-16) _____

Mind Misreading Distortion (items 17-20) _____

Misfortune Telling Distortion (items 21-24) _____

Beauty Bound Distortion (items 25-28) _____

Moody Mirror Distortion (items 29-32) _____

EIGHT UGLY ERRORS IN YOUR PRIVATE BODY TALK

Before you read about each body image error or distortion, be sure you have scored your self-test at the end of the Helpsheet. Remember, each distortion score can range from 0 to 4, with higher scores reflecting the fact that the particular type of distortion is more characteristic of your patterns of thought.

Distortion 1: Beauty-or-Beast

The Beauty-or-Beast Distortion occurs when you think about your appearance in extremes. This is called *dichotomous thinking*. Many people think about their weight in this way: "Either I'm at a perfect weight or I'm fat." A person fearful of becoming fat puts on a few pounds and concludes, "I'm such a blimp." Or, someone concerned with being too thin loses a few pounds and proclaims, "I'm just a skeleton." In a similar but less extremely polarized version of Beauty-or-Beast thinking, you consider a physical feature as either "okay, I guess" or "ugly." When being neutral, your Private Body Talk is typically quieter, because you may think along these lines: "My looks are nothing to notice; they're hardly worth thinking about."

The undistorted truth is that reality is never a matter of either-or. Reality exists on a continuum. In between black and white there are many shades of gray. As you can see, Beauty-or-Beast thinking leads you to disregard the shades of gray, and to make exaggerated conclusions about your looks.

Distortion 2: Unfair-to-Compare

The Unfair-to-Compare Distortion involves pitting your appearance against some unrealistic or extreme standard. When you compare yourself with these standards, you make yourself the loser. Magazines, newspapers, movies, television, music videos, and the Internet hit you so heavily with society's "ideal" images that you cannot escape being aware of them. Mere awareness isn't the problem, however. When you personally absorb these images, that is, when you accept society's standards as your own, you become vulnerable to the society's unreal ideals—comparing provokes despairing!

Gauging your physical worth by unrealistic ideals can cause you to fixate on your inadequacies. You focus on what you don't look like and on what you don't like about your looks. You engage in wishful thinking: "I wish I had thicker hair." "I wish I were really thin." "I wish I had a bigger chest." Your Private Body Talk will also be loaded with what I call "too" thinking. "I'm too short (or too fat or too this or too that)."

Thumbing through certain magazines, seeing some ads on television, and watching certain videos may lead you to mentally compare your appearance with how the models look. Unless you're also airbrushed or digitized to perfection (and perhaps even if you are), chances are you'll conclude that you don't measure up to the models.

This Unfair-to-Compare Distortion may take you beyond the media and mental images of perfection. You may also compare your appearance with that of real people you encounter in everyday life. However, your comparison is skewed—made only with people you judge to have the physical qualities that you wish you had. Obviously, your thoughts are biased against you from the very start. You play the comparison game, but with the rules you choose, you always lose. If you always compare yourself to a taller standard, you can only come up short.

The Unfair-to-Compare Distortion is unfair in another respect. Rarely do people pick just any physical characteristic for comparison. It's typically the one you like least, the one that bothers you most. In this way, you add insult to insecurity and make your insecurity that much worse.

Which Appearance Assumptions that you discovered in Step 4 instigate this distorted Private Body Talk? Assumption 1, "Physically attractive people have it all," heralds good-looking people as winners, so you make them a standard for self-evaluation. Assumption 8 maintains that "if I could look just as I wish, my life would be much happier." This underlying belief keeps you reviewing your ideals to see if you should be happy yet. Similarly, if Assumption 3 commands you always to look your best, you'll compare your looks to some notion of best and find ways you've not met the lofty expectation. Finally, there's Assumption 9, which complains, "My culture's messages make it impossible for me to be satisfied with my appearance." But then, you empower these media images by comparing yourself to them.

The ruminations on this mental mistake are terribly self-critical and use words like "should," "must," and "ought"; for example, "I should have a clearer complexion" or "I ought to have a smaller waist."

Furthermore, when your comparisons are with actual people, not only do you have negative feelings toward your body, but you may also experience envy and jealousy toward the people with whom you compare yourself. If you think, "They make me look bad," you become intimidated. You may try to avoid them, or gossip about them, or retaliate by giving them unwarranted grief. After all, if you could take them down a notch or two, you might be able to feel more adequate yourself. Obviously, the Unfair-to-Compare Distortion becomes unfair to everyone.

Distortion 3: The Magnifying Glass

The Magnifying Glass Distortion represents what psychologists call *selective attention*. You focus on an aspect of your appearance that you dislike and then exaggerate it—as if you're putting your body under a magnifying glass. You commit this mental error when you cannot contemplate your looks without zooming in on this one disliked feature. All you see is one huge flaw. You equate your entire appearance with your "squinty eyes," "chipmunk cheeks," "knobby knees," or "bulging butt." Your Private Body Talk is defective because all it talks about are defects. Your inner dialogues repeat themselves like a broken record. You're tired of hearing it, but you still keep playing it.

The Magnifying Glass Distortion entails underemphasis as well as overemphasis. It involves a blind mind—as you ignore or minimize your positive physical qualities. The Magnifying Glass mistake prevents you from appreciating the very features that others find most attractive about you. For example, in his Private Body Talk, a man with a handsome face says, "Oh, sure, my face is fine, but who the hell cares? Just look at this flabby mess of a body!"

One reason that some people commit this distortion is a fear of being seen as vain. They may be afraid that being pleased with their own looks would necessarily mean that they are conceited. So, if they ever catch themselves having a positive perception of their looks, their Private Body Talk zaps them with guilt and orders them to change the subject. Most often, however, this distortion derives from the bad habit of focusing on what is seen as a body image threat.

Distortion 4: The Blame Game

The Blame Game Distortion happens when you incorrectly conclude that some disliked physical attribute is directly responsible for certain disappointments and difficulties that you experience. This psychological phenomenon is called *scapegoating*. You need to blame something for your troubles, and because you already see your appearance as offensive to you, it's the convenient target.

Distorted Blame Game thinking goes like this: "If I didn't look so _____, then something (bad) wouldn't have happened." If you don't get the job or the date or the social courtesy you wanted, you readily point the finger of blame at your appearance. Your Private Body Talk alleges that your looks have stolen something you had hoped for. Your appearance stands accused, without a shred of solid evidence.

We know that a person's looks sometimes can affect life events. Being 6'8" will benefit an individual in the basketball tryouts relative to someone who is 5'7". The pretty blonde might be shown favoritism in her bid to get a public relations job. It is unfortunately true that obese individuals and those with disfiguring conditions are sometimes treated unfairly in our society. In the Blame Game, however, even in the absence of evidence, people scapegoat their appearance for any problems that may arise. After a social disappointment, it's natural to try to figure out why things happened as they did. It's clearly wrong, however, to jump to the automatic conclusion that your appearance is responsible for your disappointment.

Why are you so accusatory of your looks? Well, in Step 4, did you endorse Appearance Assumption 7—the basic belief that your appearance is responsible for much of what has happened in your life? If so, then you probably play the Blame Game often. This assumption falsely establishes a criminal record for your appearance and predisposes you to scapegoat your looks in your Private Body Talk.

In the self-test for this distortion, I asked you to imagine going to a party and meeting someone you find attractive. This happened to Terri, who was upset when the "dreamboat" left the party with another woman. Terri's Private Body Talk blamed her own appearance: "It was my flat boobs and dumb curly hair. Who'd be interested in me? I look like a stalk of broccoli!" She concluded, "It's my body's fault that he left with someone besides me. My looks aren't good enough." What Terri did not know at the time was that her "heartthrob" had left the party with his sister.

Distortion 5: Mind Misreading

Mind Misreading leads people to reason that "if I think I look bad, others must think I look bad too. They see me exactly as I see myself." The truth is other people may have entirely different ideas. Psychologists call this faulty mental process *projection*, because we project our own beliefs or thoughts into the minds of others.

In the example above, Terri also committed Mind Misreading by inferring that the fellow at the party had thought she was goofy-looking. That was her own evaluation of her appearance, which she projected into his mind. Mind Misreading and Blame Game Distortions often go hand in hand. To blame your looks for how people react (or don't react) to you, you have to presume what those people must be thinking.

Appearance Assumption 2 may propel this distortion. If you assume that your worth is defined by your looks, you place undue importance on what others may think about your appearance. If you also buy into Assumption 4, that the first thing people will notice about you is what's wrong with your appearance, you're ready to misread their minds at a moment's notice. If you're worried about your weight for example, your Mind Misreading says, "They see how overweight I am and think I'm a fat slob."

Distortion 6: Misfortune Telling

The Blame Game and Mind Misreading involve inferences about past and current events. The Misfortune Telling Distortion pertains to your predictions about how your appearance will affect your future. You predict that your physical shortcomings will have dreadful effects on your life. This may influence your expectations in short-term situations (i.e., "People at the gym will stare at me and snicker") or in the long-term (i.e., "With my looks, I'll never be taken seriously in my workplace"). Misfortune Telling uses extreme words such as "never" or "always" when you anticipate how your looks will be a detriment. For instance, you may think, "With my homely face, I'll always be unloved" or "I look so old and wrinkled that I'll never get promoted." Such sweeping expectations encompass what everybody will think about you and how they will act toward you. Face it—life and people are much less predictable than this.

What Appearance Assumptions fuel Misfortune Telling? Assumption 8 says that "if I could look just as I wish, my life would be much happier." So, the converse of Assumption 8 leads to the Misfortune Telling Distortion that unless you look exactly as you wish, your life will *never* be happy. And, of course, an implication of Assumption 7, which states that your appearance has adversely affected your past, is that your looks will surely mess up your future, too. Misfortune Telling permeates your Private Body Talk with gloomy, pessimistic predictions.

Distortion 7: Beauty Bound

The Beauty Bound Distortion is reflected in Private Body Talk that says you cannot do certain things because of your looks. This distortion imprisons you. When you limit your activities and aspirations because of your negative body image, you become its prisoner. Typical Beauty Bound thinking begins with the words "I can't." You forbid yourself to go places, do things, or be with certain people because you think you don't look good enough. You tell yourself you can't wear particular styles or colors of clothing. You deny yourself certain social or recreational activities. Your "I can't" thinking usually takes the form of "I look too _____ to do that." Sometimes, the prohibitions are temporary: "Until I get a tan, I can't go to the beach" or "Until I lose ten pounds, I can't go dancing." Other times, the Beauty Bound prohibitions are permanent: "With my hairy arms, I'll never be able to wear short-sleeved shirts" or "With my ugly body, I should never have sex."

Notice how the various Body Image Distortions often team up to create your troubles. Beauty Bound seldom operates alone. For example, a woman who decides "I can't go to the office picnic because my hair looks weird" is restricting her activities (Beauty Bound thinking) because she tells herself that people will snub her because of her looks (Misfortune Telling). A man whose Beauty Bound thinking dictates "I'm too fat, so I can't eat in front of other people" is also Mind Misreading when he concludes that others will judge him as a fat man who always overindulges with food.

Beauty Bound beliefs are fueled by several Appearance Assumptions. Return to Step 4 and reread Assumptions 5, 6, 8, and 9. Can you see how each of these assumptions can lead you to constrain your freedom of choice in living a fuller life?

Distortion 8: Moody Mirror

The Moody Mirror Distortion reflects what psychologists call *emotional reasoning*—reasoning based purely on feeling. You start with a strong emotion that you need to justify. You end up with a faulty conclusion that justifies and may even strengthen the emotion.

The Moody Mirror mistake has three variations. In its first form, your initial emotion is a negative feeling about your looks. You notice it and you ask yourself, "Why do I feel so unattractive?" Then, with very little thought, you readily answer the question, "It's because I am so unattractive." This version of the Moody Mirror Distortion follows the not-so-brilliant logic that "because I feel ugly, I must be ugly."

Here's an analogy: Imagine that you and a friend are on a leisurely walk through the park. All is serene—that is, until your friend wonders aloud if any snakes might be lurking about. Not being especially enamored of such creatures, you notice your heart is galloping. You also notice plenty of places where these reptiles might be hiding. There are logs where they could lie in wait for you. There are low-hanging branches from which they could launch an aerial assault. "This park is viper city," you conclude. "There must be hundreds slithering about. Let's get out of here!" Your fear leads you to decide that snakes must be there somewhere—despite having absolutely no evidence of them! You reasoned from your fear, inferring facts that may not be true from your feelings.

Can you apply this analogy to the Moody Mirror Distortion? Your Private Body Talk is an emotional dialogue that confuses feelings with facts: "No wonder I feel so ugly, just look at me! Look how ugly and _____ (fat, or short, or beer-bellied, or bald, or pale skinned …) I am!"

A second but related form that the Moody Mirror Distortion can take occurs when feelings of unattractiveness about one physical characteristic spill over to other features. Operating on the faulty principle of guilt by association, your Private Body Talk searches for guilty parties. As it zeros in on some unacceptable attribute, you feel unattractive and dissatisfied. Then you ask yourself emotionally loaded questions: "Just how ugly am I?" or "What else is wrong with my looks?" In answering, your mind is like a bug zapper that zaps anything coming its way. You annihilate one physical feature after another, feeling uglier each time. And the uglier you feel, the more you notice or create any imperfection in order to justify your feelings.

In the third manifestation of the Moody Mirror, you start with negative feelings about something unrelated to your looks—for example, being stressed out or in a bad mood. Then, the wildfire of your bad mood spreads and ignites your body image experiences. How can this happen? Your brain stores various Private Body Talk "tapes" that it plays and replays, producing predictable emotions. These tapes remain on pause until something switches them on. Negative emotions can set off these dormant dialogues, especially those tinged with a similar emotion, such as shame or anxiety. So your nasty mood seeks a ready target, and you unfairly malign your appearance. The Moody Mirror just looks for trouble—and really stirs it up.

THE UNDISTORTED TRUTH ABOUT DISTORTED THOUGHTS

Research confirms that people's Body Image Distortions have a strong bearing on the nature of their body image experiences. Allow me to share the results of two studies in which we measured hundreds of individuals' body image distortions using a scientific test similar to the one you took in the Thinking About Your Thinking Helpsheet. In the first study (Jakatdar, Cash, and Engle 2006), we discovered that people who had more distorted Private Body Talk had more body image dissatisfaction and distress, more investment in their appearance for self-worth, and more detrimental consequences on their body image quality of life.

In the second study (Rudiger et al. 2007), our research participants completed an extensive body image survey and then monitored their body image experiences for ten days, recording these each day in an online questionnaire. We found that those with more distorted Private Body Talk in the initial survey had many more negative body image experiences over the ensuing ten days.

Clearly, from these results, we see that these distorted thought patterns are a crucial aspect of having body image difficulties. But the findings also confirm the converse conclusion, with very positive implications. To the extent that your Private Body Talk does *not* reflect these mental mistakes, you will have a more favorable, satisfying body image in your everyday life. So let's start to work on changing your distorted Private Body Talk, no matter how problematic it is.

CORRECTIVE THINKING: START TALKING BACK

By confronting your Appearance Assumptions in Step 4, you've already begun to create a New Inner Voice. Now this voice will speak to your Body Image Distortions, so that you can change the unfair and self-defeating ways you think about your looks.

Cognitive therapists have developed highly effective strategies for changing the way you think about your experiences. These strategies are called *cognitive restructuring* or *corrective thinking*. Because corrective thinking can be difficult to learn in the midst of a distressing episode, you'll develop your corrective thinking ahead of time. Then, with a little practice, you'll be ready to apply what you've learned to alter your Private Body Talk in your daily life.

On the following pages, we'll take aim at each of the eight Body Image Distortions, one at a time. I'll give you plenty of examples to show you exactly how to talk back to your distorted Private Body Talk.

Here's what you need to do:

- First, go back in this chapter to your Thinking About Your Thinking self-test. If your score was anywhere between 1 and 4 for a particular distortion, read the specific items you found to be characteristic of your own thought patterns.

- Next, as detailed in the exercises below, read about disputing each distortion that is characteristic of how you think.

- If your score for that distortion was between 2 and 4, it's one you'll really want to work on. Underline or take note of anything in the exercises that hits home or seems potentially valuable. Afterward, it will be your turn to take aim, with the aid of the Helpsheet at the end of the section on each specific distortion.

- Based on your review of your self-test answers, pick a familiar scenario that causes you the most problems and reflects this particular Body Image Distortion. On the Helpsheet, write down the typical Activators of your body image distress. Write down the words of your Private Body Talk that commit this mental mistake. Include your beliefs, self-statements, and interpretations that reflect the distortion.

- Finally, talk back! Based on the discussion and examples of how to dispute the distortion, compose the narrative of your corrective thinking that will take issue with your distortion.

Please understand that this isn't osmosis therapy, in which you decide that just absorbing my words will be as helpful as finding your own voice. Because your New Inner Voice must talk back with your chosen words, you need to spend the small amount of time required to put your words on paper. In doing so, you are mindfully discovering, dissecting, and disputing the personal inner causes of your body image difficulties.

Correcting Your Beauty-or-Beast Distortions

Remember, Beauty-or-Beast thinking is either-or thinking: "Either I'm attractive or I'm homely." "Either I lose ten pounds or I'm fat." "Some people have it and some don't; I don't." Here are some ways to dispute such dichotomous, black-or-white ways of thinking:

- Force yourself to see things on a continuum. See the shades of gray. Remind yourself that not being a 10 on a 10-point scale of attractiveness doesn't necessarily make you a 1. Say to yourself, "Okay, so I'm not totally perfect; but I'm not totally imperfect either. I have features that enhance my appearance." Then, remind yourself of these physical assets.

- Ponder how you think about other people's looks. "Do I judge others with only two extreme categories? Or do I see them on a continuum?" If the latter, ask yourself, "Why should I view other people more fairly than I see myself?"

- Eliminate the loaded language of your thoughts by being more objective. Replace "I have a horsey face" with "I have a long nose." "I have potholes for my complexion" is, more objectively, "My complexion isn't smooth." Replace "I'm a damned scarecrow" with "I have a thin physique." "Hippo hips" becomes "rounded hips." "I'm a chrome dome" should be "I have hair loss."

- Ask yourself, "Honestly, what is the evidence, other than my own harsh judgments, that I'm seen as extremely homely?" Ask, "What is the evidence to the contrary?" Think about compliments you receive. Think about those occasions in which you felt pleased about some facet of your appearance.

Helpsheet for Change: Talking Back to My
Beauty-or-Beast Distortions

A typical activating event or situation is:

_____

_____

_____

_____

_____

_____

My distorted Private Body Talk often says:

_____

_____

_____

_____

_____

_____

_____

To correct my distorted thinking, my New Inner Voice talks back and says:

_____

_____

_____

_____

_____

_____

_____

_____

_____

Correcting Your Unfair-to-Compare Distortions

The Unfair-to-Compare Distortion comes in three forms. You pit your appearance against your own personal ideals, the media images of physical perfection, or people you find good-looking whom you encounter in everyday situations. So, you compare your appearance only with images of what you'd like to have. As a result, you spend a lot of time noticing others who you think look better than you do. And, not surprisingly, you end up feeling unattractive.

This distortion fills Private Body Talk with words and phrases like "should," "ought," "must," or "I have to be." Shame, envy, and intimidation arise from unfair comparisons. Examples of faulty Private Body Talk here are "I should be more attractive," or "I wish I were as attractive as that person is," or "That person makes me feel so ugly." Seldom do you notice that there are few people who come close to meeting your ideals for yourself.

Corrective thinking for this distortion first recognizes what you're doing. It catches you in the act of comparing yourself with somebody, leaving you upset about your looks. Use the following suggestions to let your corrective thinking set you straight:

- Replace "shoulds," "musts," and "oughts" with less demanding language. Instead of saying, "I should be better looking, taller, thinner, or ...," correctively assert, "It might be nice if I lost a few pounds, but I look pretty good the way I am. I refuse to belittle myself for not looking like a magazine cover model."

- Other helpful corrective thoughts are "I don't have to have a perfect body to have an appealing appearance." Or "Nobody's perfect; even models have imperfections that are digitally removed." Or "Nobody (but me) expects me to look different. Nobody's complaining about me but me." (If someone else is complaining about how you look, I'll help you deal effectively with his or her unhelpful comments in the Afterword of this book.)

- Be adamant in a stance that says, "I refuse to continue to buy into this societal ideal of attractiveness; it's sexist and I refuse to treat myself that way."

- The reality is that everybody is better-looking than somebody else, and everybody is less attractive than somebody else. Tell yourself, "I don't have to feel bad just because there's something about me that I don't like as much as I like what someone else has."

- Recognize that your mental compliment of someone else doesn't have to be a mental criticism of you. "The fact that I like the way a person looks has nothing to do with how I look. That person doesn't make me look bad; he or she doesn't make me do anything."

- Your New Inner Voice says, "Okay, if I'm going to compare, then I need to be fair. So, whom am I more attractive than?"

- Finally, say to yourself, "I'm going to take time now to think of something else about me (a special skill, talent, or personality trait) that compares quite favorably with other folks."

Helpsheet for Change: Talking Back to My
Unfair-to-Compare Distortions

A typical activating event or situation is:

_____

_____

_____

_____

_____

_____

My distorted Private Body Talk often says:

_____

_____

_____

_____

_____

_____

To correct my distorted thinking, my New Inner Voice talks back and says:

_____

_____

_____

_____

_____

_____

_____

_____

_____

_____

Correcting Your Magnifying Glass Distortions

When you view your looks through the distorted Magnifying Glass, you focus on what you don't like and minimize the attributes that don't cause a problem. You take a tunnel-vision perspective on yourself. When you think about your loved ones, do you think only about their weight, warts, or wrinkles? Of course not! You have a fairer, more balanced picture of their looks and who they are as people. Freed from this distortion, your Private Body Talk will reflect a more balanced view of your looks and yourself.

- Begin by asking yourself, "Am I dwelling on what I don't like and forgetting about those parts of me that are fine?" When you magnify, you can correct your mind's eyesight by saying to yourself, "I'm just focusing on my dislikes and that's not the whole picture. I do like (for example) my expressive eyes, my warm smile, and if I say so myself, I do have good hair."

- Say to yourself, "I may not like my _____ (hair, hips, muscles, etc.), but other people see more to me than the feature that I'm hassling myself about."

- Just as you do to correct the Beauty-or-Beast Distortion, replace pejorative statements about magnified attributes with less demeaning descriptions. "Small-chested" is more accurate than "flat as an ironing board."

- When you start self-criticizing in the mirror, interrupt your thoughts and say, "I caught myself picking on myself again. I'm going to stop, give myself a smile, walk away from this mirror, and say something accepting of myself."

- Promise to abide by the Equal Time Rule, which states that you should spend an equal amount of time on your likable features or traits whenever you catch yourself mentally harping on what you dislike about your body.

Helpsheet for Change: Talking Back to My Magnifying Glass Distortions

A typical activating event or situation is:

_____

_____

_____

_____

_____

_____

My distorted Private Body Talk often says:

_____

_____

_____

_____

_____

To correct my distorted thinking, my New Inner Voice talks back and says:

_____

_____

_____

_____

_____

_____

_____

_____

_____

Correcting Your Blame Game Distortions

The Blame Game makes the mistake of *misattribution*. That occurs when you too quickly infer that your appearance is responsible for some disappointment or other undesirable event. Examples of Private Body Talk based on playing the Blame Game are "I don't have a boyfriend because I'm so unattractive" and "People are unfriendly to me because I'm balding."

To correct Blame Game thinking, you first must realize that blaming your looks for unfortunate events usually involves jumping to conclusions based on a guess—a biased guess. What's the real evidence? If you objectively examine the facts, often the only evidence that indicts your appearance is your own discontent with your looks—hardly convincing proof.

How can you talk back to the Blame Game?

- Sometimes all you need to do is catch yourself blaming your looks, see that you have no evidence for your conclusion, and tell yourself, "Stop blaming!" Then, move on to more important things—like being friendly or having fun. Or you could say to yourself, "Here I go again, blaming my looks for ruining everything. I'm going to leave my appearance out of this and focus on what I can do to make things better."

- Your New Inner Voice is a voice of reason and says, "I know I'm probably blaming my looks simply because I don't like them. That doesn't mean my looks are actually causing anything bad to happen."

- Blaming isn't sufficient evidence to warrant a conviction. Ask yourself, "Okay, what real evidence do I have that my appearance is to blame for this? What other explanations are there?"

- Suppose you do have reasonably good evidence that your looks really did cause the problem; for example, you asked someone out for a date and the person declined, giving your looks as the reason. So what? Not everyone will like everything about your looks. For that matter, not every person you meet will like your car, your clothes, your politics, or your religious beliefs. One person's opinion is not everyone's opinion. If a few folks reject you because of such reasons, it may be their problem, and their loss! There are some judgmental, prejudiced people in this world. If you're overweight and someone is hatefully biased against overweight people, this person is not rejecting you; he or she is rejecting an entire category of people. Do you really need to be concerned about what such a bigoted person thinks about you? Say "Adios" and move on.

Helpsheet for Change: Talking Back to My Blame Game Distortions

A typical activating event or situation is:

_____

_____

_____

_____

_____

_____

My distorted Private Body Talk often says:

_____

_____

_____

_____

_____

_____

To correct my distorted thinking, my New Inner Voice talks back and says:

_____

_____

_____

_____

_____

_____

_____

_____

_____

Correcting Your Mind Misreading Distortions

Mind Misreading happens when you project your own thoughts about your looks into the minds of others. You leap to the incorrect inference that other people see and judge your appearance in the same way that you do. Then you fill their heads with your own thoughts. You think, "Everybody who sees me is thinking about my _____ (large ears, acne, big breasts, short stature, or whatever)."

As I mentioned earlier, Mind Misreading often occurs in tandem with the Blame Game Distortion. Suppose, for instance, that your Private Body Talk is blaming: "My partner didn't want to have sex last week because he or she is turned off by my awful body." While you condemn your looks as the reason for sexual "rejection," you reached your verdict only by Mind Misreading. How do you know that your partner's thoughts about your looks led to a lapse of interest in sex? Could it be that your partner was simply not in the mood or was preoccupied with work? Besides, did you make it clear you were interested in sex? If not, why did you expect your partner to read your mind and know that you were feeling amorous?

The strategies for handling Blame Game thinking are also useful in managing Mind Misreading. Here are more ideas to help you "keep your thoughts to yourself":

- First, accept what you're doing—you're thinking about what someone else might be thinking about you. Do the thoughts and opinions you suspect others are having about your looks strangely resemble your own opinions? If you're being presumptuous, simply admit that you may be Mind Misreading.

- Accept reality: Say to yourself, "I'm fairly bright, but I can't read minds. The only mind I'm reading here is my own."

- Do you have any evidence that contradicts what you presume another person is thinking? If it's someone you know well, has the person ever made positive or affirming comments about your looks? Has he or she ever disagreed and reassured you when you complained about your appearance?

- Ask yourself, "If my appearance isn't what bothers people, what else could it be?" Among alternative explanations, consider several that are often true. People aren't likely to be warm and amiable if you are not friendly. Could you have been acting cool and distant because of your worry that others won't like you or your looks? Also, others may be shy or having a bad day. Could their behavior mean that something is wrong with them—not with you?

- Talk back assertively to your Private Body Talk when it is disparaging: Say to yourself, "I need to stop thinking about what others may be thinking. Instead, I need to change what I am thinking."

Helpsheet for Change: Talking Back to My Mind Misreading Distortions

A typical activating event or situation is:

_____

_____

_____

_____

_____

_____

My distorted Private Body Talk often says:

_____

_____

_____

_____

_____

_____

_____

To correct my distorted thinking, my New Inner Voice talks back and says:

_____

_____

_____

_____

_____

_____

_____

_____

_____

Correcting Your Misfortune Telling Distortions

The Blame Game charges your appearance with past or current offenses, but Misfortune Telling distorts your thinking about the future with pessimistic predictions that bad things will happen because of your looks. Your Private Body Talk uses words like "always" or "never." For example, consider this thought: "I'll always be a misfit because of my looks." Misfortune Telling can also distort expectations about specific situations, such as "I'll have a terrible time if I wear this bathing suit at the beach" or "Once my boyfriend sees me naked, our relationship will end." Can you detect the Mind Misreading that's happening here?

When correcting this faulty thinking, you should again see that you are jumping to conclusions in the absence of evidence. How do you really know that your worst fears will come true? Separate your emotions from your judgments of your future. Here are some helpful ways to do that:

- Realize that your pessimism may actually stem from the expectation that you'll feel self-conscious in some situation. In fact, your discomfort is probably the worst thing that will happen. So quit making dire predictions and start finding ways to accept feeling some self-consciousness in the situation.

- When you think, "I'll never be loved because of my appearance," realize that what you may really be feeling is this thought about your future: "I'm worried that I won't be loved." But by definition, your future hasn't occurred yet; it's your experience of despair or apprehension that's occurring. If you focus on feeling more accepting of your appearance, you'll feel less apprehensive. Tackle other worries separately.

- Analyze the evidence. Have your pessimistic predictions always come true? Think about instances in which events turned out more favorably than you'd expected. What did you do to make a difference?

- Listen to your New Inner Voice say, "I'm going to quit worrying about the future and concentrate on now. What can I do now to prove my doom-and-gloom predictions wrong?" The answer, of course, is to live your life with the opposite assumption: "My future is up to me!"

Helpsheet for Change: Talking Back to My Misfortune Telling Distortions

A typical activating event or situation is:

_____

_____

_____

_____

_____

_____

My distorted Private Body Talk often says:

_____

_____

_____

_____

_____

_____

To correct my distorted thinking, my New Inner Voice talks back and says:

_____

_____

_____

_____

_____

_____

_____

_____

Correcting Your Beauty Bound Distortions

When you think, "I can't do that because of my looks," you are engaging in the Beauty Bound Distortion. This is a hazardous distortion because it can set self-fulfilling prophecies in motion. For example, imagine you tell yourself you're too fat to go to the pool party. Misfortune Telling and Mind Misreading drive you to make this Beauty Bound mistake in your thinking. So, you pass on the party and sit at home wallowing in self-pity, lamenting that your "loathsome looks" have robbed you of a good time—again! Of course, your looks didn't deprive you of anything, your emotional decision did. Beauty Bound Distortions also create catch-22 situations like "I can't go to the gym and exercise to lose weight until I lose weight."

Later, in Step 6, I'll teach you some terrific behavioral techniques to overcome the limits you allow Beauty Bound thinking to set for you. Until then, here are some ways to talk back to this distortion:

- Ask yourself, "So why *can't* I do such-and-such?"—for instance, "I can't go to the class reunion unless I lose twenty pounds." Why not? Will there be a sign posted that says, "Heavy Folks Not Admitted Under Penalty of Law"? Your answer is "Because I am self-conscious about my weight and will worry about what others are thinking." Dispute your Misfortune Telling and Mind Misreading mistakes. It's your own discomfort stopping you, not your looks or what other people are truly thinking.

- Talk back to "I can't do it" by asking, "How can I do it? What would make it easier to do?" For example, "I can't go to the mall with this haircut" becomes "I can go if I wear my favorite hat." Replace "I can't go to the gym until I lose weight" with "I can go to the gym if I remind myself that facing my anxiety is an act of admirable courage."

- Face the fact that other people, who are far from being perfect physical specimens, engage in the same activities that you deny yourself. Do they all really look better than you? Or do they refuse to deprive themselves of involvement in life simply because they aren't perfect? Will you really have the only imperfect body at the gym or the pool party?

- Think about other times in which you've accomplished things that you first felt insecure about until you gave yourself a little push, took them on, and mastered them. Didn't it feel good to prove to yourself that you could overcome obstacles and succeed? Remember those occasions and tell yourself you can do it again.

- When you are ruled by the Beauty Bound Distortion, how do you feel? Frustrated? Angry? Dejected? Imagine how you would feel if you stood up to "I can't" by saying, "Oh yes I can." Imagine that you face your apprehension and do it anyway. How would you feel? More confident? More in control?

- Counter your Beauty Bound pessimism with motivating experiences. Apply the wisdom conveyed in the inspirational, not-just-for-children book *The Little Engine That Could*. Affirm to yourself, "I think I can! I think I can!"

Helpsheet for Change: Talking Back to My Beauty Bound Distortions

A typical activating event or situation is:

_____

_____

_____

_____

_____

_____

My distorted Private Body Talk often says:

_____

_____

_____

_____

_____

_____

To correct my distorted thinking, my New Inner Voice talks back and says:

_____

_____

_____

_____

_____

_____

_____

_____

Correcting Your Moody Mirror Distortions

The final distortion is the Moody Mirror mistake, which involves emotional reasoning. It can happen in several ways. When you are "feeling ugly," you take your negative emotion as proof that you are ugly. You search for any or all things about your looks that might justify your feelings. This distortion can also occur when you're in a bad mood or upset about something other than your appearance; your funky mood contagiously infects your Private Body Talk. Moody Mirror thinking triggers other mental mistakes, activating one distortion after another and carrying you from one criticism to another, in waves of feverish distress.

Corrective thinking treats the spreading infection. The key is to understand that your bad mood came first, and you conveniently pointed to your looks to rationalize your distress. Other people with identical physical "flaws" do not necessarily feel as bad as you feel. An inferiority complex doesn't exist in the same genetic material that gave you a short stature or a receding hairline or extra cushioning on your butt.

How often have you heard people belittle their own looks, while your impression of their appearance was not as negative as theirs, and perhaps not negative at all? A friend may say to you, "My hair looks terrible," yet objectively you can see that it looks fine. Or you hear a woman say, "My hips are as big as a buffalo's," and knowing how big buffalo hips really are, you ignore her comment as an exaggeration much larger than her hips. You're not that person, so you can be unemotionally objective. You know that the individual's actual appearance isn't really the problem—even if your friend's hair could look better or the woman's hips could be smaller. The problem is what the person believes and feels.

The following corrective thinking tactics can temper your Moody Mirror mistakes:

- Approach the Moody Mirror by thinking as an unbiased, objective observer would. Catch the distortion as soon as you notice your mood and before the discontent spreads. Like a snowball rolling down a hill, the farther it goes, the larger and more forceful it becomes. Stopping it is much easier at the top of the hill than near the bottom. Realize that obsessing over your physical imperfections doesn't fix what's wrong. The obsessing is what's wrong.

- Ask yourself this: "Was something else already bothering me before I started worrying about or criticizing my body?" Then say, "Okay, my appearance isn't really the issue here. I need to accept that my day was really stressful and I'm going to leave my looks out of this."

- Use a mental stop sign to halt your Private Body Talk. Listen to your New Inner Voice say, "I'm not feeling very attractive right now. This isn't a good time to contemplate my looks. I'm just making myself feel worse. So I'm going to stop this!" Step away from this Private Body Talk (after a brief apology, of course, to your body for the false accusations). Then follow the Equal Time Rule, and compliment yourself.

- Suppose you've upset yourself by criticizing the way your hair looks. Then you begin to insult your weight. Stop right there! Mindfully catch yourself and say, "Okay, I'm at it again. Being discontent with my hair is no reason to pick on other things about my looks."

- Replace "I am" thoughts with "I feel" thoughts. For example, replace "I am awful looking in this sweater" with "I feel less happy with this sweater than I'd like to be."

- Fixating on feelings often intensifies them, like dwelling on a headache's sensations intensifies your pain. So mindfully notice your feelings, accept them, and then pull yourself out of the emotional quicksand and turn your attention to something that can create different feelings. Watch a funny video, visit your favorite Web site, listen to upbeat music, or take an invigorating walk.

- Your New Inner Voice obeys this variant of an old saying: "If I can't say anything nice about myself, I won't say anything at all." Then shift gears!

Helpsheet for Change: Talking Back to My Moody Mirror Distortions

A typical activating event or situation is:

_____

_____

_____

_____

_____

My distorted Private Body Talk often says:

_____

_____

_____

_____

_____

_____

To correct my distorted thinking, my New Inner Voice talks back and says:

_____

_____

_____

_____

_____

_____

_____

_____

MAKING YOUR NEW INNER VOICE A NATURAL PART OF YOUR LIFE

By working with the Helpsheets for Change, you've helped your New Inner Voice find words to begin to create inner experiences that are free of painful distortions. This is an important beginning of more accepting Private Body Talk. Of course, the crucial issue is that you are able to carry out corrective thinking in the here-and-now events of everyday life.

A Mindful Mind-Set: Stop, Look, and Listen

In Step 3, you learned how to mindfully attend to and accept your thoughts and feelings as inner experiences—nothing more and nothing less. From Steps 4 and 5 you learned how to change your problematic Private Body Talk in daily life. Now, whenever you have negative feelings about your looks, you know how to Stop, Look, and Listen. First, you *stop* reacting, judging, and fretting. Second, you become mindful of your inner experiences—as you *look* at your thoughts and emotions objectively and accept that they exist and are only what they are. Finally, you *listen* to your New Inner Voice—a more reasonable, realistic, nonjudgmental point of view. Now, you can talk back to yourself with your New Inner Voice and correct your troublesome thinking. You can talk to yourself just as you would to a good friend who's said the same unfair, critical things about himself or herself that you've just privately said about yourself—and that you know aren't true.

Your New Body Image Diary

It's time to exchange your Body Image Diary, which you began using in Step 3, for a new, expanded version. You will still enter the A-B-Cs as before—the *Activators* of your body image discomfort or distress, the *Beliefs* inherent in your Private Body Talk, and the emotional and behavioral *Consequences* of these experiences. What's new in your New Body Image Diary is that you will add a *D* and an *E*. D stands for the *Dialogues* expressed by your New Inner Voice—how you correctively dispute Distortions and Appearance Assumptions that you detect in your Private Body Talk. E refers to the *Effects* of your New Inner Voice on your emotions and your actions. E identifies your improvements as a result of changing your Private Body Talk. From now on, use this New Body Image Diary to record the A-B-C-D-E sequence of your body image experiences.

Copy the New Body Image Diary at the end of this chapter, or simply use its format in the journal or notebook that you are using. From now on, each and every day, try to keep a record of your challenging body image experiences and how your New Inner Voice has handled these challenges.

Helpsheet for Change: My New Body Image Diary

Activators:

_____

_____

_____

_____

Beliefs:

_____

_____

_____

_____

Consequences:

_____

_____

_____

_____

Dialogues of my New Inner Voice:

_____

_____

_____

_____

Effects of my New Inner Voice:

_____

_____

_____

_____

FINAL WORDS OF ENCOURAGEMENT

There are some important things to keep in mind as you work to strengthen your New Inner Voice in your everyday life. Your first attempts at corrective thinking may seem odd or unnatural, they may not fit quite right, like a new pair of shoes. That's certainly understandable. Your New Inner Voice may not sound like you. Don't worry; it will become a better fit soon.

Typically, human change is gradual. Don't expect that corrective thinking will cause your body image difficulties to disappear immediately and totally. Initially, your new corrective thinking will mostly prevent your distress from getting out of hand, so appreciate that "less bad" is good. And new events or situations may necessitate finding different words for your New Inner Voice, so be flexible and be innovative. I remember a client who, after a few days of corrective thinking, complained that he still hated his body. He concluded "Either this program doesn't work or, if it does, I'm a hopeless case." Eventually, however, after becoming more patient with himself, he saw that both of his explanations were untrue—the program did work for him and he was not a hopeless case. So be tolerant, and accept any tough times as expected "bumps in the road." Never give yourself a hard time for having a hard time. That only makes it worse. And you don't deserve worse! Accept that you are where you are. Don't judge it.

It's a fact of life that people are more likely to behave in ways that are rewarded and rewarding than in ways that aren't. Rewarding yourself for mindfully monitoring your body image experiences and for corrective thinking is crucial. Mentally recognize your efforts and commend your successes. Mindfully do something special to affirm yourself in your quest to improve your body image quality of life. Buy yourself some fresh flowers, treat yourself to a movie, or take an invigorating walk. In a later chapter (Step 8), I'll show you even more positive ways to promote your improvements.

Facing Your Body Image Avoidance

Marlena is miserable. She hates her body and is firmly convinced that her "pear shape" is the only thing anyone ever notices about her. Every day of her life is filled with bouts of self-consciousness and efforts to avoid or escape these unpleasant feelings. She never accepts her friends' invitations to pool parties or workout sessions with them at the gym. Dark outfits that hide her hips and thighs are the only clothes she wears. Having sex with her fiancé is very unpleasant, because she is extremely anxious about him seeing her body, so she keeps the bedroom dark and always wears a loose-fitting nightgown. She'd prefer to avoid the "whole ordeal." Because Marlena is also embarrassed by the freckles on her face, she routinely applies a thick cover-up cosmetic to conceal her complexion before leaving the house. Her motto seems to be "What they can't see can't hurt me." But if she were right, why would she hurt so much?

SELF-DEFEATING SELF-DEFENSES

With Steps 4 and 5, you began changing the faulty mental assumptions and distortions that provoke and perpetuate your painful body image experiences. In Steps 6 and 7, you'll learn how to change certain troubling behavior patterns. People engage in all kinds of efforts to manage their appearance and to deal with their disturbing Private Body Talk. From monitoring the ABC Sequence of your own body image experiences, you've probably observed that you try to avoid certain Activators that set off your discomfort. Among your Consequences, you may discover patterns of specific self-protective actions you take to manage your misery once it's begun.

Body image distress, whether actually experienced or merely expected, usually will set in motion behavior patterns for self-defense. These maneuvers are efforts to correct, conceal, or compensate for what you think is wrong with your looks. However, these habitual behavior patterns create their own problems. They stir up their own distress and then, paradoxically, are used to cope with the difficulties they've caused. Unfortunately, these well-learned patterns reinforce your conviction that your looks are somehow defective. Put simply, your self-defenses are self-defeating.

So why do you continue to do such things? The answer is self-protection: You want to avoid or escape feeling bad about your looks. You develop these behaviors to protect yourself, so that bad events either won't happen or, if they do, so that they won't be nearly as unpleasant as they might be. Psychologists call this learning by *negative reinforcement*. This is entirely different from learning by *positive reinforcement*, in which we do things because doing them rewards us with positive outcomes and pleasurable emotions.

Thus, self-protective actions are motivated more by preventing discomfort and emotional pain than by providing pleasure. With these actions, you either try to hide (avoid, disguise, or flee) the "problem" or you compulsively seek ways to make it go away. These two patterns of behavioral self-defense—hiding and seeking—are called *Evasive Actions* and *Appearance-Preoccupied Rituals*.

Now, look back at your Body Image Coping self-test results in Step 1. Two of the scores are indicators of the extent to which you use these two self-defeating behavior patterns to deal with threats or challenges to your body image. How high were your Appearance Fixing scores and your Experiential Avoidance scores?

Figure 6.1 shows how these self-protective patterns emerge in the flow of your body image experiences. With your Appearance Assumptions setting the stage, events trigger your distorted Private Body Talk and your resultant body image discomfort or distress. To manage these negative thoughts and emotions, you engage in action to defend against or cope with these experiences. I want you to understand that such patterns of self-protection are really acts of self-rejection. You are rejecting the acceptability of your body, which worsens both your body image and your self-esteem.

In Step 6, first you'll discover your own Evasive Actions and then you'll learn how free yourself from these self-defeating avoidant behaviors. In Step 7, you'll identify your Appearance-Preoccupied Rituals and learn how to rid your life of these problematic patterns. So, let's get going with self-discoveries.

DISCOVERING YOUR EVASIVE ACTIONS

Often, people with a negative body image will go to great lengths to avoid displaying their "defects," not only to others but to themselves, as well. There are two basic kinds of Evasive Actions—running and hiding. Let's examine them.

Running

If you go back and review your Body Image Distress Test from Step 1 and the entries in your Body Image Diary, you'll probably find various situations and activities that you run from. When you engage in the Beauty Bound Distortion, you forbid yourself to do certain things because of your looks. You avoid these things because they threaten you with feelings of self-consciousness, shame, anxiety, or embarrassment.

What you avoid falls into one or more of the four categories of the four P's: practices, places, people, and poses. Each of the following four sections has a checklist of some of the things that people

Figure 6.1. The Role of Self-Defensive Actions in Your Unfolding Body Image Experiences

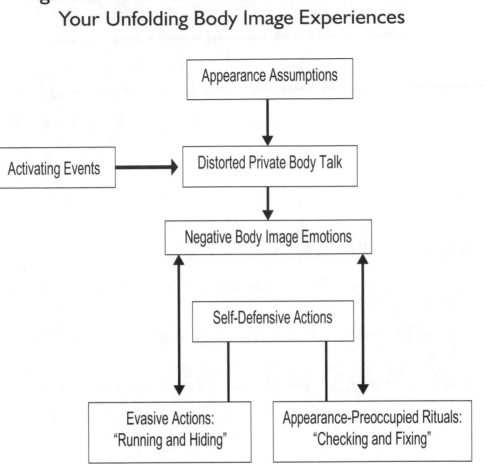

may avoid. If an item applies to you, check it. Then, based on your answers, write down what you personally avoid in the Self-Discovery Helpsheet: My Evasive Actions below. Feel free to include any of your Evasive Actions that are not in these checklists.

DO YOU AVOID CERTAIN PRACTICES?

☐   Wearing clothes of a style, color, or fabric that might reveal your "flaws."

☐   Some physical activity that might call attention to your body's appearance—such as exercising, dancing, or playing certain recreational sports.

☐   Some normal activity in which somebody might see you when you are not "fixed up"—such as going to the grocery with sweats on, or going out without makeup or with your hair not done.

❑   Some activity that might "mess up" your appearance—for example, an activity like swimming that would wet your hair or wash off your makeup.

❑   Paying attention to your body—for example, weighing yourself or viewing your mirror reflection or a photo of yourself.

❑   Allowing your partner to see you in the buff.

❑   Certain physical contact—such as giving or receiving hugs—that might disclose to others how your body feels.

❑   Being photographed or videotaped.

❑   Eating heartily in the presence of others—for fear they'll think you're fat.

DO YOU AVOID CERTAIN PLACES?

❑   Any place where your body is relatively exposed—such as at the pool or beach, or dressing rooms and public showers.

❑   Places where appearance is emphasized—such as dressy formal occasions or singles' gatherings.

❑   Clothing stores where your appearance is "on display" to clerks or customers.

❑   Places with prominent mirrors—such as department-store dressing rooms or exercise classes in mirrored rooms.

DO YOU AVOID CERTAIN PEOPLE?

❑   People who are good-looking in ways you'd like to be.

❑   Good-looking members of the sex you are attracted to.

❑   People who do a lot of things to "look good"—for example, people who diet, exercise regularly, or wear stylish clothing.

❑   Individuals who talk a lot about physical appearance.

❑   People who might comment on your appearance—usually a friend or relative who's inclined to make unwelcome comments about your weight, manner of dress, and so forth.

DO YOU AVOID CERTAIN POSES?

❏   Where or how you sit or stand during a social interaction—for instance, stances or profiles that might "spotlight" your disliked characteristics (e.g., body shape, posture, hair, or facial features).

❏   Gestures that you think make your "defects" more pronounced—such as smiling (and exposing disliked teeth, dimples, or wrinkles) or hand gestures (which show "stubby" fingers or chipped or bitten fingernails).

❏   Particular positions during sexual relations—notably those that allow your partner to see the parts of your body that you dislike.

Hiding

Hiding is an Evasive Action in which people try to protect themselves against negative body image thoughts and feelings by using various grooming behaviors to conceal or camouflage what they dislike about their looks. Certain Appearance Assumptions that you uncovered in Step 4 can lead you to disguise what you despise. That is, if you assume that your unadorned appearance is unacceptable and will taint others' impressions of you, you'll probably want to hide what you really look like.

The trappings of bodily adornment can act as mood-altering substances. People select clothing, jewelry, cosmetics, and hairstyles either to feel attractive (positive reinforcement) or to feel less unappealing and to shield their shortcomings from others (negative reinforcement). Of course, the latter is a self-protective way of Grooming to Hide. How do people groom to hide?

Well, the skinny guy wears long-sleeved shirts and long pants all year round to cloak his arms and legs. The heavy-hipped woman shrouds her shape with dark, loose-fitting shirts and slacks. The aging woman conceals her wrinkled face under layers of makeup. The balding fellow hides beneath his hat. The man with protruding ears veils them with his long hair. The woman with small breasts wears padded bras. The lady with dark hair growth on her face or arms bleaches it. And God forbid that her gray hair should show. She conceals it with hair-coloring. This list could go on and on.

Now, think about your own physical characteristics that trouble you. What do you do to hide them so they'll be less apparent to others or for you to feel less concerned about them? Add these behaviors to your Self-Discovery Helpsheet: My Evasive Actions.

Self-Discovery Helpsheet: My Evasive Actions

List what you do to avoid negative thoughts and feelings about your looks. Then, rate how often you engage in each Evasive Action on the scale of 1 to 3 below.
1 = on occasion; 2 = fairly often; 3 = very often

How Often   Practices

_____   _____

_____   _____

_____   _____

_____   _____

                             Places

_____   _____

_____   _____

_____   _____

_____   _____

                             People

_____   _____

_____   _____

_____   _____

_____   _____

                             Poses

_____   _____

_____   _____

_____   _____

_____   _____

                             Grooming to Hide

_____   _____

_____   _____

_____   _____

_____   _____

Facing Avoidance

Now, having identified the self-defeating, avoidant behavior patterns that are linked to your negative body image, it's time to learn how to take control of them, instead of allowing them to continue to control you. There is a lot of substantial scientific proof that people can overcome their anxieties by gradually exposing themselves to whatever they avoid because of anxiety. Of course, what is really avoided is an inner experience (i.e., thoughts and emotions) that they find uncomfortable or unacceptable. One very effective way to manage your Evasive Actions is to use an active strategy called *Facing It.*

You have already acquired most of the skills you need to face down your Evasive Actions. You've learned how to mindfully observe and accept your inner experiences, without judging them or reacting to them. You've also cultivated your New Inner Voice—an essential ally for Facing It. Now, I'd like to teach you a few additional skills that can help you manage the tension or discomfort that is likely to come from Facing It.

LEARNING BODY-AND-MIND RELAXATION

Several fairly simple techniques to calm yourself physically and mentally can really help you face what you no longer choose to avoid. These build nicely on your capabilities of mindfulness and acceptance. It is an indisputable fact that relaxation is the physiological and psychological opposite of distress. You cannot be uptight or upset and be "cool, calm, and collected" at the same time. Body-and-Mind Relaxation techniques will enable you to become more comfortable and to bring to a halt any runaway train of negative body image thoughts and emotions. Spend a few days learning and rehearsing the following three exercises so that you can put them into practice whenever you need them.

Letting Go of Tension

When you're troubled or distressed, your brain sends messages that signal your muscles to contract. Because these messages are stored in those muscles, your muscular tension can linger and you may stay vulnerable to emotional negativity about your body image or even to something completely unrelated to your body image. Here's how you can counter such messages:

- First contract (tense) and then relax your muscles, one set at a time, for each of these four sets of muscles: (1) face, neck, and shoulders; (2) hands, forearms, and biceps; (3) chest, stomach, and lower back; (4) buttocks, thighs, calves, and feet.

- Inhale as you are tensing for each set of muscles for about three seconds. Slowly exhale as you release the tension.

- Be mindfully aware of exactly how the tension feels and how your body feels as you release or let go of the tension.

- Each time you release tension, mentally repeat the phrase "letting go."

- With repeated practice, you can simply tell your body to "let go" of any specific muscular tension that you've noticed, without having to go through the tense-and-release sequence.

Diaphragmatic Breathing

When under stress, your breathing becomes irregular and leads to physical sensations that further undermine feelings of control or contentment. With deep, rhythmic *diaphragmatic breathing*, however, you can enhance experiences of relaxation and contentment.

- Lie down and, reclining comfortably in a quiet, private location, gently close your eyes.

- Take five slow, deep breaths. Preferably, inhale through your nose and exhale through your mouth. Breathe evenly from your diaphragm, which is the lowest part of your chest at the top of your abdomen. Breathe so that your stomach slowly rises and falls, while your chest moves only slightly. You can put one hand on your stomach and the other on your chest to verify this.

- Be mindful of the sensations caused by the air flowing in and flowing out of your body. Be aware of your abdomen rising and falling. Be aware of the sounds of the flow of your breathing.

- Engage in this exercise for about ten minutes, or longer if you wish. Practice diaphragmatic breathing a few times a day for several days.

Mental Imagery

When fretting about your appearance, it's likely that you replay frustrating or upsetting situations in your mind. These mental images evoke negative emotions. Being able to shift your attention away from distressing images and to turn on pleasant ones cultivates inner serenity.

- With your eyes closed, allow your imagination to paint a pleasing picture of a landscape in your mind. Using your imagination, simply place yourself in a springtime scene, at the beach, in the mountains, or in the countryside—whichever pleases you most.

- Begin to paint your mental picture vividly and then experience your pleasant scene as if you were really there.... You hear the songs of birds, singing so sweetly.... You see the colors of nature around you.... You feel the soothing, gentle warmth of the sun.... Against your skin you feel a soft breeze that caresses your body...

- Mindfully enjoy your pleasant scene.... For about ten minutes allow its details to unfold and envelop you in experiences of contentment and peacefulness.

Building Your Ladder of Success for Facing It

Here's what you need to do to get ready for Facing It:

- On the Evasive Actions you listed in your Self-Discovery Helpsheet: My Evasive Actions, above, review the practices, places, people, and poses that you avoid because of past experience or future expectation of discomfort. (Hold off on the Grooming to Hide items; we'll deal with those later.)

- Make a simple judgment about each situation or activity that you avoid. This is a judgment that psychologists call *self-efficacy*. Self-efficacy is your degree of confidence that you could actually enter the situation or engage in the activity. For instance, suppose that you avoid going swimming at the community pool because you feel self-conscious in a swimsuit and have too many thoughts that you look unattractive with wet hair. Ask yourself, "How confident am I that I could actually take a dip in the pool?" Your answer is your level of self-efficacy for this activity.

- Assign each item on your Evasive Actions list a self-efficacy rating from 0 to 100. A rating of 0 means "No way. Never in a zillion years would I be able to do that." A rating of 100 says "I'm 100 percent certain that I can do that." A 50 means there is a fifty-fifty chance that you could Face It. Write down your self-efficacy level in the margin next to each of the avoided practices, places, people, and poses.

- Next, you will design a Ladder of Success. Transcribe the items and their self-efficacy ratings to the following Helpsheet for Change: My Ladder of Success for Facing It. Put the hardest items (those with the lowest self-efficacy ratings) at the top of the ladder and the easiest ones (with the highest ratings) at the bottom.

- Make sure your list contains a reasonable range of ratings, though about half should be under 50 (that is, fairly difficult). If two or more items have the same numerical rating, decide which is a little more difficult and list it on a higher rung. If an activity or situation is very general, be more specific. For example, "eating in front of others" might become "having hors d'oeuvres at Paddy's Pub with my friends." Drop any item that isn't practically feasible. For instance, you can't go to the beach if it's below freezing outdoors right now.

- If all or nearly all of your items are rated below 50, yours is a hard-to-do list. If most are rated above 50, it's an easy-to-do list. Try to even out a lopsided list by adding a few more Evasive Actions, either easy or hard, or by modifying the existing ones to make them more or less difficult to do.

Helpsheet for Change: My Ladder of Success for Facing It

Self-efficacy ratings are from 0 for no confidence to 100 for complete confidence.

Self-Efficacy Rating

What Am I Going to Face?
(practices, places, people, and poses)

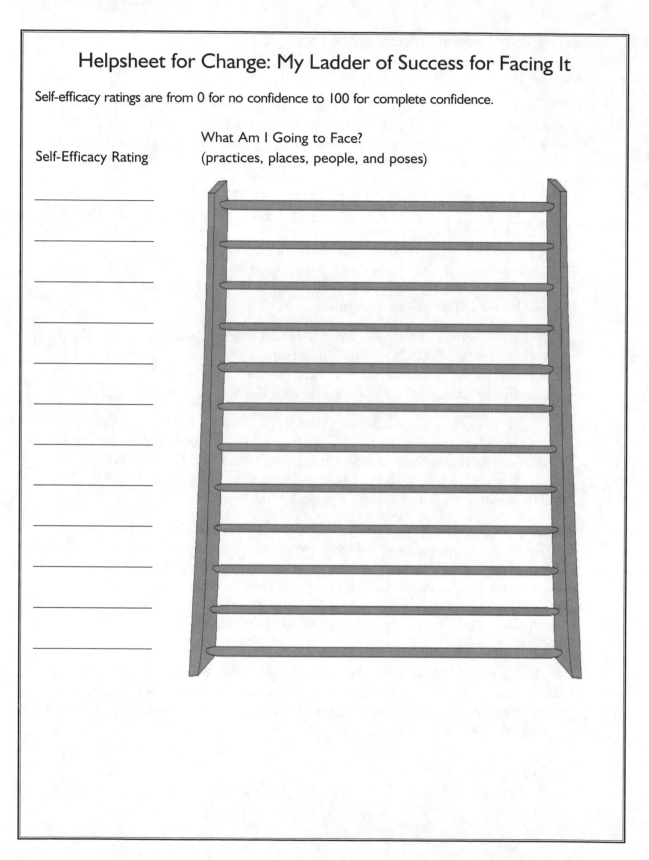

_____

_____

_____

_____

_____

_____

_____

_____

_____

_____

LEARNING TO PACE YOURSELF

Next, you will engage in the practices you avoid, go to the places you avoid, be with the people you avoid, and strike the poses you avoid. You'll do this gradually, one step at a time. You'll start out at the lowest rung on the ladder—the easiest one to do. Success at each step will give you the confidence to move up the ladder to master more difficult experiences.

Of course, you are apprehensive about facing these uncomfortable situations. Otherwise you wouldn't be avoiding them in the first place, right? So you may already be talking to yourself about what you're not going to do. Be aware of your resistance but don't retreat! Together we'll formulate a positive plan of action so that you will be victorious over avoidance.

Facing It always has four fundamental steps: (1) Prepare, (2) Act, (3) Cope, and (4) Enjoy. The first letters of these four steps remind you to PACE yourself. Here's how it works.

Prepare

You'll Prepare for Facing It by writing down your strategy in advance. This first step is crucial, as it involves you in planning and rehearsing the remaining three steps. Decide exactly what you're going to do and when you're going to do it. Figure out how you will talk back to your Old Inner Voice of avoidance that says, "No, I can't. Not now. I'll do it some other time." By anticipating which pessimistic thoughts are likely to run through your mind and how they might make you feel, you can decide how you'll handle them. Finally, you can promise to reward yourself for your efforts at Facing It. Decide ahead of time what your reward will be—a special treat, some affordable trinket, a cone of tasty frozen yogurt, or a relaxing moment with your favorite music. Having first spelled out this detailed plan using the Helpsheet for Change: My Ladder of Success for Facing It, rehearse it in your mind.

Act

The time has arrived to Face It—to carry out your plan. To warm up cold feet, give yourself the pep talk you've prepared, engage in a moment of Body-and-Mind Relaxation, or do whatever else will help you follow through. You can be mindfully aware of your inner experiences of anxiety and your impulses to avoid, and can accept these experiences without allowing them to control your actions. And off you go! As you begin confronting what you've so often avoided, encourage and commend yourself. Good for you!

Cope

When uncomfortable thoughts and feelings rise up, that should come as no surprise attack. You expected them, and you know how to accept them. Just draw upon the coping skills you've learned and roll with any discomfort. For example, you can use your New Inner Voice or elements of Body-and-Mind

Relaxation, such as calming imagery or breathing techniques. Reassure yourself that you can handle this. Remind yourself that you are handling it. Stay in the moment of what you are accomplishing.

Enjoy

There, you Faced It! But don't forget the deal. Facing It earns a reward. Applaud your accomplishment, don't criticize it. Never say "Yes, but" to yourself by saying "Yes, I did it, but..." Just enjoy your success. Relish your reward. You deserve it.

Preparing Your PACE Plans

The My Plan for Facing It Helpsheet that follows this section is for developing your PACE plan of action for each item on your ladder. Make copies of this Helpsheet and fill them out as you climb each rung of your Facing It Ladder of Success.

- Develop your first plan. Start at the bottom rung of your ladder, with the activity or situation that you're reasonably confident you can face. **P**repare by drafting your plan for Facing It.

- Decide how you will **A**ct. Specify the place, date, time, duration, and frequency of your action. For example, suppose your Evasive Action is "I avoid standing anywhere that people are behind me and can see the shape of my rear." Your action plan might be "Each day at work for the next five days, at 10 A.M. and at 4 P.M., I'll spend at least two minutes at the file cabinets where my coworkers can see me from behind."

- Now write down your plans to **C**ope. Remember, your goal is not to be totally free from discomfort while facing what you normally avoid. Your goal is just to carry out the activity, to accept any discomfort you feel as natural, and to comfort yourself. So, in my example, you must understand that when you stand at the file cabinet you will accept your self-consciousness rather than fight it and you will use pleasant imagery and particular corrective thinking to create other experiences of the situation.

- What's the reward you'll **E**njoy afterwards?

Helpsheet for Change: My Plan for Facing It

Practice, place, people, or pose avoided: _____

_____

Step-by-Step Plan for Facing It

Prepare: Exactly what will I do?

_____

_____

_____

Act: When? Where? For how long?

_____

_____

_____

Cope: What uncomfortable thoughts and feelings do I expect? How will I accept and cope with them?

_____

_____

_____

Enjoy: How will I reward my efforts?

_____

_____

_____

What were my results of Facing It?

_____

_____

_____

Implementing Your PACE Plans

Okay, you've prepared your plan by writing it out on the Helpsheet. Now what?

- After you've prepared your plan by scripting it, rehearse it. Mentally review exactly how you will act, cope, and enjoy. Visualize yourself carrying out each step of your plan. Then... Ready... Set... Go! Execute your plan. Act... Cope... Enjoy!

- As you move up the ladder, if an item seems too hard to do, break it down into simpler steps. For example, the situation "having my partner see me naked" might begin with your partner seeing you in your underwear. There's no need to get totally naked until you're ready.

- Focus on the current rung of your ladder. Don't worry about the rungs you haven't prepared for yet. You'll handle those when you get there. Don't be like the guy who has trouble doing high school geometry because he starts worrying that he'll never be able to learn college calculus.

- After each accomplishment, however small, make a note of what worked best and record the results on your Helpsheet.

Onward and upward!

COMING OUT OF HIDING

With the second type of Evasive Action, you Groom to Hide what you dislike about your looks. However, your "cover-up" is experiential avoidance—your self-protective strategy to avoid having negative thoughts and feelings. The Facing It approach to changing these behaviors is identical to the strategy used to confront the activities and situations that you avoid.

Building Your Facing It Ladder for Grooming to Hide

Previously, at the bottom of the Self-Discovery Helpsheet: My Evasive Actions, you listed your maneuvers for hiding whatever it is that you don't like about your appearance. By now, you probably know what to do next: You will use the following list to develop your Ladder of Success for Facing It on the next Helpsheet.

- First, rate your confidence in your ability to refrain from using each particular action to conceal your looks.

- Organize and fine-tune your ladder from the bottom (the easiest item with the highest self-efficacy level) to the top (the hardest item with the lowest self-efficacy level).

- Because your Grooming to Hide takes place in a range of contexts, pick specific situations to work on. For example, suppose that you listed "I always wear heavy foundation makeup to conceal my pale complexion," or "I usually wear long, baggy tops to hide my tummy," or "I always wear baseball caps or hats to hide my hair loss." For each of your Grooming to Hide behaviors, think of a couple of situations in which you could conceivably not do these things. Select common everyday situations like walking around at the mall, going to class, or getting coffee at your local café. Choose situations in which not engaging in your Grooming to Hide behavior is reasonably acceptable for anyone. Nobody's asking you to attend church services in your bathing suit.

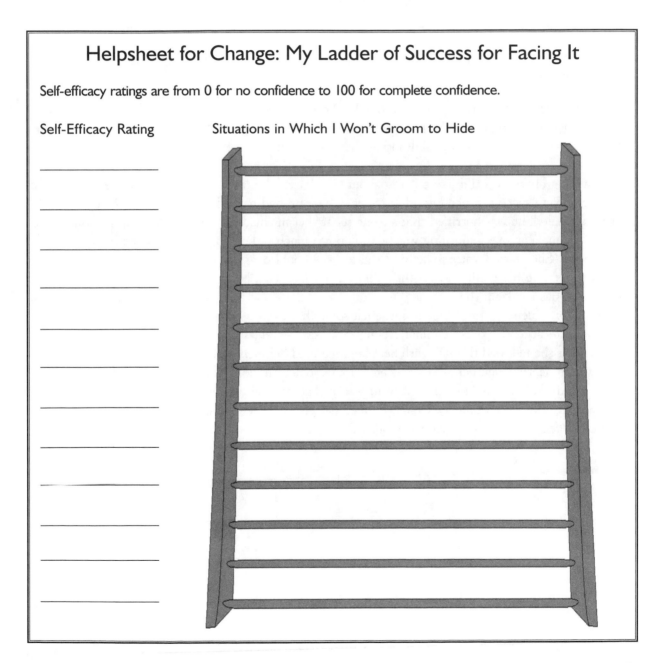

Helpsheet for Change: My Ladder of Success for Facing It

Self-efficacy ratings are from 0 for no confidence to 100 for complete confidence.

Self-Efficacy Rating   Situations in Which I Won't Groom to Hide

PREPARING AND EXECUTING YOUR PLANS FOR COMING OUT OF HIDING

Having constructed your Ladder of Success, here's how you will "blow your cover" and come out of hiding:

1. Start with the bottom item and PACE yourself. Use a copy of the Helpsheet for Change: My Plan for Facing It, which follows this section, to write down on paper how you will **P**repare, **A**ct, **C**ope, and **E**njoy the success. Mentally rehearse each aspect of your plan.

2. Afterward, carry out your plan, and acknowledge and write down the results.

3. As usual, move up to the next rung, and the next rung, and the next, all the way to the top of the ladder.

Before long, you'll see that your sense of self-efficacy and your ability to PACE yourself have become much stronger. Avoiding and hiding are becoming patterns of the past. Now, Facing It seems more like a game—a game of challenge and skill rather than one of chance and risk. And in the end, you'll be a winner!

Speaking of winners, I'd like tell you about Charlotte, who faced one of her Evasive Actions and enjoyed complete success. Since her adolescence, Charlotte had never left home without wearing layers of facial makeup. She was horrified that anyone seeing her might think she looked plain or homely. But applying her makeup every morning was taking up too much of her time. So, she constructed her plan for Facing It. She started with something she felt she could do—go outside, without makeup, to her mailbox to retrieve her mail. She did this every day for five days. Next, she went for a walk at a nearby park wearing less makeup than usual. Then, on five occasions wearing fewer and fewer cosmetics, she biked to a convenience store. Of course, she felt somewhat nervous and self-conscious each time.

Charlotte accepted these familiar feelings and did not allow them to deter her. Her discomfort diminished as she followed through with her plan. She used her mental imagery skills and her New Inner Voice to calm herself when her anxiety became troublesome. Charlotte capitalized on her love of exercise and was mindful of how invigorating the walk and the bike ride felt. After each trip, she rewarded herself by listening to Mozart. Ultimately, Charlotte freed herself from the necessity of hiding behind a mask of cosmetics. It felt so good to be able to be herself!

Helpsheet for Change: My Plan for Facing It

How I Groom to Hide: _____

_____

Step-by-Step Plan for Facing It

Prepare: Exactly what will I do?

_____

_____

_____

Act: When? Where? For how long?

_____

_____

_____

Cope: What uncomfortable thoughts and feelings do I expect? How will I accept and cope with them?

_____

_____

_____

Enjoy: How will I reward my efforts?

_____

_____

_____

What were my results of Facing It?

_____

_____

_____

FINAL WORDS OF ENCOURAGEMENT

Changing your Evasive Actions requires courage, commitment, and your acceptance of momentary discomfort. These behavioral changes are likely to be your most life-changing accomplishments. Doing away with the self-defeating habits of falsely protecting yourself from your own thoughts and emotions is a change that promotes your body acceptance and your self-acceptance. Facing It takes time, planning, risk taking, and patience. You need to accept your own imperfections while making these changes. Don't give up. Giving up is an act of avoiding failure, but of course it doesn't really work because nothing changes. Nothing gets better. Savor your successes, however small, because one small change makes the next one easier and more likely! In the next Step of this workbook, you will learn how to change your Appearance-Preoccupied Rituals, which also undermine your ability to accept your body.

Erasing Your Body Image Rituals

Greg suffers from *androgenetic alopecia*. Don't worry, it's not a deadly disease. Greg just has normal male-pattern balding—mostly a receding hairline and some thinning hair on the crown of his head. But it drives him crazy. So what does he do? He counts each hair lost forever as it swirls down his shower's drain. He mousses and meticulously combs the remaining strands over the visible part of his scalp. He scrutinizes his scalp in the mirror from every possible vantage point. He has tried dozens of different brands of shampoo that promise thicker hair. Often when he's out, Greg has the urge to check his hair to see if it looks okay, so he'll search for public restrooms with mirrors or look for reflective surfaces. While driving, he frequently (and dangerously) inspects his hair in the rearview mirror. If Greg isn't satisfied that his hair looks acceptable, which is often the case, he will wear one of his many baseball caps all day long.

Denise is a fashion plate. Whatever she wears, it is always chic and well coordinated. Her hair and makeup are impeccable. Her friends often tell her how great she looks. Most people would assume that Denise derives immense satisfaction from being so attractive. But she doesn't. In fact, she regularly ruminates that she doesn't look "right." Each morning getting ready for the day takes her two hours. When dressing for a social event, she changes clothes three, four, even five times. Each outfit seems to reveal to her something "awful" about her body. Because she worries that her thighs are huge and that her stomach sticks out, Denise must find an outfit that won't betray her "ugly secrets." Often, she'll try on older clothes that are a size smaller than she wears to see if they will magically fit again. She's terrified of gaining any weight, diets constantly, and nervously weighs herself and pinches her tummy (her "fat check") several times a day.

DISCOVERING YOUR APPEARANCE-PREOCCUPIED RITUALS

Appearance-Preoccupied Rituals were introduced in Step 6 and depicted in figure 6.1. In addition to Evasive Actions, they are a second type of self-defeating body image behavior. These rituals are repetitive efforts at body image damage control. When these patterns have been established, people compulsively inspect and check and recheck their appearance and seek remedies to fix whatever they believe might be wrong with their looks. Individuals trapped in such rituals spend inordinate amounts of time and effort to "look right."

Unlike the self-conscious avoiders of mirrors, people like Greg and Denise practically live in front of their mirrors, fussing over and "fixing" every perceived flaw. Their Private Body Talk constantly nags them about how they look, and they need reassurance, from themselves or others, that they look okay (or better). Appearance-Preoccupied Rituals come in two forms—*Checking* and *Fixing*.

Appearance Checking

Checking Rituals are often preceded by recurrent thoughts that something is wrong with your looks. This preoccupies you and makes you ill at ease. Your Private Body Talk has an answer for its nagging notion that you might not look just right: "Gotta check it out!" So, to quiet your restless mind, you check it out.

Let me offer an analogy. When you're tucked in bed and dozing off to sleep, has the question "I wonder if I locked the door?" ever crossed your mind? You may be 99.9 percent certain that you did. But the question lingers and you can't put it to rest. So, what do you do? Yes, you get out of bed and check whether the door is latched. It is. Now you can start counting sheep. The worrisome rumination in your mind is called an *obsession*. The checking behavior is a *compulsion*. Because acting on the compulsion quiets the obsession, the pattern is reinforced. The next time the preoccupying thought occurs, the stronger the urge is to act out the checking behavior.

The principal aim of Checking Rituals is to seek and obtain relief from unsettling worries about your appearance. Checking Rituals are sometimes willful, deliberate attempts to avoid worrying. At other times, they are mindlessly automatic reactions, because they've become well-practiced habits.

Some signs of this pattern are listed below. To what extent does each example describe you? Place a check mark next to the descriptions that fit fairly well.

- ❑ You have intrusive thoughts that tell you to inspect your appearance. These thoughts are hard to dismiss until you've acted on them.

- ❑ If you pass a mirror (or other reflecting surface), you often reflexively check to make sure that your appearance is okay.

- ❑ You frequently visit the restroom with the conscious intent of checking your appearance, even though you have no good reason to believe that something is really wrong with your looks.

❑   If concerned about your weight, you frequently weigh yourself to find out if you've gained or lost any small amount. Whenever scales are available, it's hard to resist weighing yourself.

❑   If concerned about your body weight or shape, you often pinch or squeeze areas of your body to try to determine how fat or thin they are.

❑   You routinely check out other people's opinions about your looks to seek reassurance that you look fine. Trusted loved ones or friends are typically asked, "Do you think I look okay? Are you sure? Are you really sure?"

❑   In social situations, you repeatedly check how your appearance compares with what others look like, so that you can feel more certain that your appearance is acceptable.

Now, based on the items in the checklist above, describe your own Checking Rituals. Write these down in the top section of the Self-Discovery Helpsheet: What Are My Appearance-Preoccupied Rituals? that you will find following the section "Appearance Fixing," below. Add any Checking Rituals that you engage in that may not have been mentioned. In describing your personal pattern, be specific.

Appearance Fixing

Fixing Rituals, which usually coexist with Checking Rituals, involve elaborate and meticulous efforts to manage or modify your appearance. You must do a lot of things with a lot of precision to be satisfied that you look okay. Special social situations may demand even more time and perfection in figuring out what to wear. If something doesn't appear (or feel) quite right, you may start your fixing all over again. How frustrating!

Recall that your Appearance Fixing score on the Body Image Coping self-test in Step 1 offers a partial index for this behavior pattern. Here's a more specific checklist of some telltale signs of Appearance-Preoccupied Fixing Rituals. Think about each one and decide how often you become fixated on fixing.

❑   At home, getting out of the bathroom and getting dressed on time is a rare event.

❑   Friends or people in your household have remarked on the amount of time you spend on your appearance. Their comments may range from gentle kidding to irritation at having to wait for you to get ready.

❑   You primp and fuss with your clothes, hair, and/or makeup more than you think you should. Rationally, you know you look fine. Emotionally and behaviorally, you just can't leave well enough alone.

❑   Different situations demand that you change what you're wearing. Otherwise, you worry that your appearance might be inadequate or inappropriate.

❒ You purchase clothing or grooming products that you seldom wear or use. When you bought them, you were sure that they were what you needed to enhance your looks. Ultimately, they didn't fully meet your expectations.

❒ Before going out, you change clothes or redo your hair several times until you're satisfied that you look okay.

❒ When you see yourself in a mirror or other reflecting surface, you reflexively adjust some aspect of your appearance—like your hair, your tie, or your dress—even though nothing is really amiss.

❒ You regularly make significant modifications in your appearance—for example, changing hairstyles or hair colors or getting cosmetic makeovers.

❒ Gaining a couple of pounds or the experience of feeling fat compels you to go on a diet or to exercise more intensely for a few days.

Now, based on your answers above and any other Fixing Rituals you engage in, write these down in the following Self-Discovery Helpsheet for Change: What Are My Appearance-Preoccupied Rituals? For both your Checking and Fixing Rituals, rate how often each behavior occurs.

ERASING RITUALS

Let's be sure we keep things in proper perspective. Managing your physical appearance is definitely a good thing. We bathe, shave, do our hair, and clothe and adorn ourselves in ways that make us feel comfortable and are esthetically pleasing. Only people with problems like severe depression or schizophrenia may completely neglect their physical hygiene and appearance. Later, in Step 8, we'll consider how these activities can represent positive ways in which we relate to our bodies. In contrast, when we are dealing with Appearance-Preoccupied Rituals, we've lost control and are really struggling not to feel bad about ourselves.

Like Evasive Actions, we experience our rituals as what we *must* do to avoid thinking and feeling that something about our looks (and worth as a person) is flawed, wrong, inferior, unacceptable, imperfect, judged negatively by others, and so forth. Because checking and fixing temporarily calm our concerns, we keep doing them, despite the clear or partial realization that they are preoccupying and seem to have a life of their own.

This reminds me of the story about the fellow who regularly went out into his front yard, surveyed the premises with his binoculars, then flapped his arms like a duck, turned in a circle, did a little dance, and spit three times over his left shoulder. A curious neighbor finally approached him to ask him what he was doing. Somewhat nervously, he replied that he was keeping the elephants away. Perplexed, the neighbor said, "But there are no elephants around here." The fellow smiled proudly and said, "I know. What I do really works!"

I hope you can see that Appearance-Preoccupied Rituals also fuel false assumptions—for example, if you don't look perfect all the time, bad things will happen or people won't like you. To change these

Self-Discovery Helpsheet: What Are My Appearance-Preoccupied Rituals?

List your Appearance-Preoccupied Rituals below, and rate how often you engage in each:
1 = not more than once or twice a week; 2 = about once or twice per day; 3 = several times per day.

Ritual Frequency   My Checking Rituals

_____   _____

_____   _____

_____   _____

_____   _____

_____   _____

_____   _____

_____   _____

Ritual Frequency   My Fixing Rituals

_____   _____

_____   _____

_____   _____

_____   _____

_____   _____

_____   _____

_____   _____

_____   _____

habitual patterns, you can either prevent yourself from initiating them or interrupt them once you've begun the ritual. I call this solution *Erasing It*. It derives from *exposure and response (or ritual) prevention*, a well-known and effective behavior therapy procedure. Several successful strategies exist for Erasing It. I'll describe each and illustrate its helpful use.

Obstructing Your Rituals

Most Appearance-Preoccupied Rituals occur whenever the "right" opportunity arises. Given certain triggers, or Activators in your ABC Sequence, you carry out the behavior before you know it. Therefore, you may need to obstruct its opportunity to occur. You block its path.

- Think about one Appearance-Preoccupied Ritual for which you need certain "tools" or conditions to carry out the ritual. For example, you require a mirror for rituals in which you repeatedly scrutinize your looks. Compulsive weighing would be impossible without scales. How could you make trouble for your ritual by altering the environment? Developing this strategy is a challenge to your creativity. So be creative!

- This obstructive technique for change is usually a short-term, stopgap approach. You don't want to avoid one thing in order to avoid another. It can be helpful, especially at first, but note that you'll want to use additional strategies to remove most rituals.

Allow me to illustrate this point: Lois felt compelled to weigh herself almost every time she ate anything. She was ill at ease until she confirmed that she had not put on several pounds. So Lois applied masking tape to the weight-displaying window of her scale. She obstructed her ritual's path. In this way, she weakened her compulsion to weigh herself. She combined this technique with the By Appointment Only strategy (discussed below), weighing herself only on Saturdays, when she changed the tape. Lois's innovative strategy helped her to change her preoccupying mental tape, as well.

Delaying Your Rituals

Another method for Erasing It is really simple. You learn to wait a while before commencing your ritual. This works quite well for Checking Rituals.

- Appearance checking is usually preceded by an inner urge to check. For example, you may have a gnawing feeling that you "need" to weigh yourself, inspect your hair or makeup, or seek reassurance about your looks. Your urge is typically narrated by your Private Body Talk that asks "What if?" and conjures up distressing scenarios. "What if I've gained weight and I look fat?" "What if my hair is out of place and looks really messy?" "What if my makeup is wearing thin and my big pores are showing?" "What if my husband thinks this outfit looks dumb on me and he's ashamed to be seen with me?" Just be mindfully aware of these urges and mental what-ifs. Accept that they occur and let your consciousness move away and focus on other things.

- Checking Rituals serve several self-protective purposes: They interrupt your preoccupied thoughts and your feelings of discomfort. Moreover, they offer a clear answer to your what-if? question. When you learn that you look fine, you feel relief. And, if something was slightly amiss, fixing it brings relief. So, you'll want to detach the thoughts from the ritual. You are aware that you want engage in the checking behavior. You remind yourself that it isn't required that you do so.

- By postponing your checking even for a short time, you sap the power of your anxious urge. Instead of succumbing to the urge and letting it immediately dictate your actions, you become the decision maker. You take control of deciding when (or whether) to check on your looks. This usurps the urge that instigates your ritual, as well as the ritual itself. So, for example, you decide "I'll delay checking for ten (or fifteen or thirty) minutes."

- Waiting it out will be uncomfortable for a while, so you'll need to accept the discomfort and create mindful experiences to soothe yourself during your wait.

You can learn from the following success story: Roger is a sales representative for a pharmaceutical firm. He's on the road a lot, calling on doctors and clinics. During the course of a typical day, he checked his appearance often. Every time he stopped at a traffic light, he inspected his hair and face in the rearview mirror. At his office, he checked his appearance once or twice an hour, using a mirror he kept in his desk drawer or the one in the men's room.

When Roger decided to delay his rituals, he put off checking his reflection in the rearview mirror until he reached his destination. Whenever he had the urge to check his appearance at the office, he deferred checking for twenty minutes. At first the waiting troubled him—what if he looked awful all that time? However, he just mindfully observed and accepted his worried thoughts. Next, he spent a few moments doing slow, diaphragmatic breathing and listening to his encouraging New Inner Voice. Then, he more easily shifted his attention to his work. Eventually, Roger kept his urge to check in check.

Restricting Your Rituals

Fixing Rituals can be exasperating for others. Each fixing episode usually continues until you are either momentarily content with its results or you run out of time. An alternative to allowing your ritual to run its course is to place specific limits on it. Here are three ways to weaken your rituals by placing specific limits on them:

PLAYING BEAT THE CLOCK

Here's how you could tackle a Fixing Ritual in which you take too long readying your appearance to face the world.

- First establish how long your Fixing Ritual usually takes.

- Then make a fair estimate of how much time would be reasonable for you to take if you didn't get so compulsively caught up in it. For example, suppose your morning grooming regimen takes two hours. You know that if you were a bit more organized and less picky, you should be able to get ready in one hour. At first, set your initial goal generously—say, to be ready in one hour and fifty minutes.

- Set your alarm clock or kitchen timer to this limit and play Beat the Clock.

- After a few days of success, lower the limit—say to one hour and forty minutes—and play Beat the Clock for several more days.

- Continue in this fashion, shaving off ten minutes each time you change your limit, until you've reached the reasonable amount of time to groom that is your goal.

- Reward your progress by using the time saved to do something enjoyable. Then you'll appreciate the change even more.

Kyra liked her hair, but she insisted that it always had to look perfect. Her hair was the "saving grace" she relied on to make up for the physical features she disliked. Dreading a bad hair day, each morning Kyra would style and restyle her hair for about an hour, until her ride for work arrived. For two weeks, she played Beat the Clock by setting her timer for gradually shorter intervals—forty-five minutes, then thirty, and finally a reasonable twenty minutes. Her goal was to be finished with her hair, out of the bathroom, and enjoying her cranberry juice before the timer alarm went off. By making a challenging game of it, Kyra eliminated her morning preoccupation with her hair, which looks just as attractive as it did back in the days of one-hour fixing sessions. Now if she has a bad hair day, she sticks to her new abbreviated schedule anyway. She knows that the world won't come to an end.

RATIONALLY RATIONING RITUALS

This next method sets a limit on the number of times you engage in a ritual within a certain period. How does this work?

- Suppose that whenever you go out to dinner with a friend or loved one, your requests for reassurance that you look fine begin to sound like a broken record. The more you ask, the more insecure you feel, especially if you start to sense your companion's annoyance. So, you set a quota and allow yourself only two reassurance requests during an entire evening.

- You can use your allocation whenever you wish, but having used up your ration, your requests are over.

- Over time the goal is to set your ration progressively lower until it reaches zero.

BY APPOINTMENT ONLY

Here's the third method for restricting your rituals:

- An intense urge to practice a ritual usually dictates when your rituals will take place. So instead, put those rituals on a schedule. In effect, you make an appointment with yourself to carry out your ritual.

- Like any appointment, the one for your ritual should begin and end on time.

- Because you're permitted to have the ritual by appointment only, it cannot occur at unscheduled times. If you miss your appointment, you must wait for the ritual's next scheduled occasion.

Here's an example of an effective use of this strategy: Since adolescence, Ivan's face has been prone to blackheads. Many times a day, he would get out his magnifying mirror and peruse his pores in search of blackheads and blemishes, squeezing and picking at them. Not only did these search-and-destroy missions take a lot of time, they took their toll on his complexion as well. To gain control, Ivan scheduled an appointment for his ritual, allowing it to take place only during ten-minute visits to the mirror at 7 A.M. and 7 P.M. Thus, he restricted his ritual's duration and frequency. Much to his dermatologist's relief, Ivan eventually reduced his unhealthy practice to once a week.

Resisting by Rebellion

This last strategy for Erasing It can be rather difficult, yet sometimes it is the most successful. You rebel against your ritual by resisting it cold turkey. You face the temptation and exercise restraint. You ride out your urge without performing the ritual. Controlling a ritual, despite the conditions being ripe for its occurrence, can greatly increase your self-confidence.

- You may want to try this approach first on weaker rituals. For stronger ones, you'll probably graduate to this approach after successfully delaying, restricting, or obstructing your behavior pattern.

- With mindful acceptance, Body-and-Mind Relaxation, and corrective thinking as your allies, you force yourself to remain in the situation where you experience the urge without performing your ritual—the longer the better.

- Often a gradual approach is most helpful. Schedule your rebellions for progressively longer periods. In this way, you build up your resistance.

- In other instances, it may be effective for you to remain in the situation until the urge to perform your appearance-preoccupied pattern has subsided. You mindfully observe the urge and its weakening.

- If you try this total rebellion against the ritual and don't succeed, give yourself the credit you deserve for trying. Never give yourself a hard time for having a hard time!

Take inspiration from Jessica, who learned how to resist two self-defeating patterns: Whenever she was on a date, Jessica spent almost as much time in the restroom checking and fixing her appearance as she spent with her companion. She would end up stuck to the mirror the way a magnet sticks to a refrigerator, brushing her hair, freshening her makeup, and adjusting her clothes.

But once Jessica made up her mind to end her appearance checking and fixing, she planned her resistance well. On several occasions when she was at a restaurant, she allowed herself to visit the restroom only to use the toilet, not to primp. When washing her hands, she made a point of looking down at the sink instead of up at the mirror. For her next step, Jessica required that, on each visit, she look at herself in the mirror—but not fix anything. She progressed to longer and longer periods between "checkups." Relying on her mindfulness and coping skills to get her through her initial discomfort, Jessica was finally able to break her pattern of checking and fixing.

BUILDING YOUR LADDER OF SUCCESS FOR ERASING IT

Now it's your turn to take the first steps toward weakening your Appearance-Preoccupied Rituals. Erasing It requires you to do some creative planning to devise a strategy appropriate for yourself. Once you've settled on a strategy, execute it frequently to erase your old pattern.

- Go back to the Self-Discovery Helpsheet: What Are My Appearance-Preoccupied Rituals? earlier in this chapter, where you listed your Checking and Fixing Rituals. Read through your list and evaluate how confident you are that you could refrain from the behavior if you were in the situation where it normally occurs. Just as you did in Step 6 when you were preparing to change your Evasive Actions, assign each entry on your list a self-efficacy rating from 0 to 100. This indicates how confident you are that you will be able to refrain from each Checking or Fixing Ritual.

- Arrange these rituals in order of self-efficacy on the following Helpsheet for Change: My Ladder of Success for Erasing It, going from the highest rating at the bottom to the lowest rating at the top.

Helpsheet for Change: My Ladder of Success for Erasing It

Self-efficacy ratings are from 0 for no confidence to 100 for complete confidence.

Self-Efficacy Rating   Checking or Fixing Rituals That I Am Going to Erase:

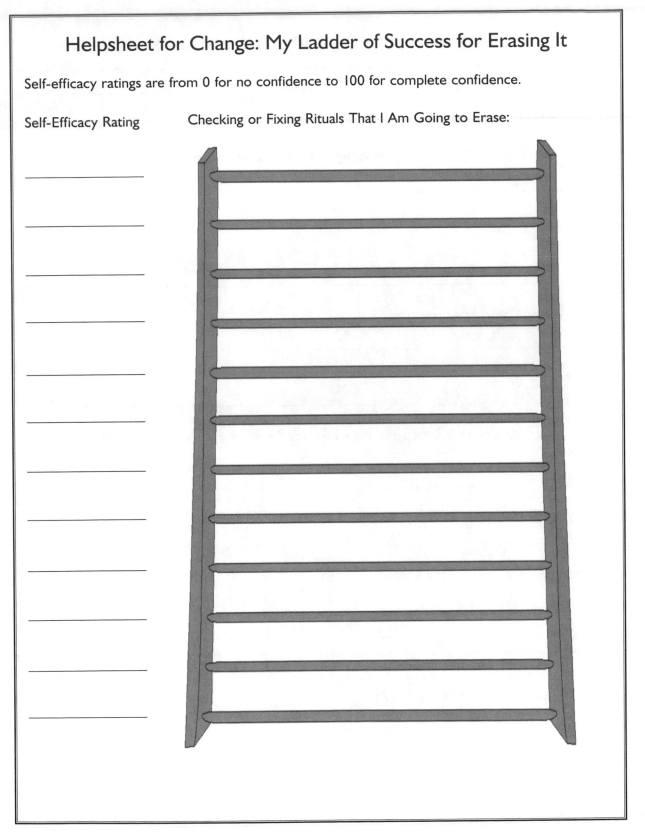

Helpsheet for Change: My Plan for Erasing It

My appearance-preoccupied Checking and Fixing Ritual: _____

_____

Step-by-Step Plan for Facing It

Prepare: Exactly what will I do?

_____

_____

_____

Act: When? Where? For how long?

_____

_____

Cope: What uncomfortable thoughts and feelings do I expect? How will I accept and cope with them?

_____

_____

_____

Enjoy: How will I reward my efforts?

_____

_____

_____

What were my results of Facing It?

_____

_____

_____

Preparing and Executing Your Plans for Erasing It

- Start with the ritual at the bottom—the easiest one to eliminate. Write out your plan for Erasing It, using the Helpsheet for Change: My Plan for Erasing It. You'll want to make several copies of this Helpsheet to use for each ritual, or you can use your own notebook to write out your plan in this format.

- PACE yourself, just as you do when Facing It to manage your Evasive Actions. As you plan, anticipate and specify each step—Prepare, Act, Cope, and Enjoy. Visualize yourself carrying out your plan, coping effectively with any troubling thoughts or feelings, and affirming and enjoying your accomplishment.

- You've made and rehearsed your plan for Erasing It. Now go for it!

- One rung at a time, just keep climbing your ladder. When you've made headway with several Checking or Fixing Rituals, go ahead and begin Step 8 of this workbook. Continue to follow through on your Erasing It plans.

FINAL WORDS OF ENCOURAGEMENT

The behavioral changes you make by doing the work of Steps 6 and 7 represent important strides in your journey toward body acceptance. They enable you to shed your old self-defeating habits that are fruitless efforts to protect yourself from uncomfortable inner experiences. As you continue to work on these changes, I want you to face forward and imagine your life free from Evasive Actions and Appearance-Preoccupied Rituals. Close your eyes and take about fifteen minutes to picture this new life clearly and in detail. Mindfully immerse yourself in this vision. How is your life different? How does it feel to be rid of these behaviors? How do you feel about yourself?

Treating Your Body Well

All human relationships involve a fundamental exchange of actions and reactions between people. We exchange both positive and negative giving and receiving. In satisfying romantic relationships or friendships, we feel that the giving and the getting are balanced fairly. Positive, rewarding exchanges greatly exceed and overshadow negative, punitive exchanges. Good times can redeem bad times.

In unhappy relationships, giving and receiving are out of balance, and negative exchanges outweigh the few good times. One common complaint is "I'm not being treated right. I deserve better than this!" Discontent can range from resigned disappointment to raging anger and resentment. Whether in self-protection, protest, or retaliation, each person tends to react in ways that make the relationship deteriorate even further. But quietly withdrawing and avoiding or ignoring one's partner won't restore troubled relations to a better balance. Angrily demanding better treatment and punishing your partner for not providing it only make matters worse.

POSITIVE BODY-SELF RELATIONS

So, perhaps you are wondering, what does all this have to do with body image? Well, your body image does involve a relationship—between you and your body. If it's a frustrating, unhappy one, the "gives and gets" seem unjust and the exchanges are distressing and demeaning. You then react in ways that worsen rather than affirm and enhance your relations with your body. Understanding how you mistreat your "body-partner" is essential to turning this relationship around.

Thus far in this workbook, the principal emphasis has been on changing your negative interactions with your body. By correcting your distorted Private Body Talk, you deescalate the critical assaults and accusations you direct at your body-partner. You are also working on becoming less demanding of perfection and more accepting of your body-partner's shortcomings. By Facing and Erasing your self-defeating patterns of behavior, you are becoming less obsessed with your frustrating and resentful efforts to fix or control your body-partner.

These are necessary changes, but they aren't enough. As with all satisfying human relationships, a successful body-partnership requires more than the absence of bad times. Have you ever felt fulfilled by a friendship solely because your friend didn't belittle you? How many people do you know who are happily married only because their spouses don't berate them? The truth is that good things happen in good relationships. They thrive as the result of affirming and rewarding experiences, not just because of a lack of distressing ones. In Step 8, the final step of this workbook, you'll learn how to add good times to your relationship with your body.

If you wanted to improve a troubled relationship with a friend or relative, I would counsel you to create new shared experiences. I would tell you to put aside complaints from the past and to concentrate on the present. Both of you would commit to doing what you know you have to do to make things better—even if you don't feel like doing it. You would stop the mutual finger-pointing and say to one another, "I'm truly sorry. I know I haven't treated you well. I want to start fresh. I want to be as good to you as I can." Each of you would say, and affirm, something like this: "In the future, rather than being so faultfinding, I'm going to remind both you and myself of what I value in you."

TAKING AFFIRMATIVE ACTIONS

Affirmative Actions are vital to improve your relationship with your body. These actions involve doing special things to foster positive body image thoughts and feelings. With conscious, mindful effort, you can counteract the quagmire of your previous negative experiences and start anew. To get started, first you need to make amends with your body.

Writing Wrongs

When thinking of your body as you would a friend, you can reach only one conclusion: You've mistreated your friend. In this exercise, you will write your body-partner a letter expressing your wish to set your relationship on a better course. In your letter, using the following Helpsheet, you will apologize to your body-partner for your prior mistreatment, express assurances that you want to change, and thank your body-partner for the good things it has given you.

Write this letter as you would write to an estranged friend with whom you want to restore relations. When you finish writing, keep your letter nearby, perhaps taped to your bathroom mirror. Put it somewhere that you will not fail to see it. It will be a reminder of your new attitude.

Right now you may be thinking, "You want me to do what? Write a letter to my body? That's weird!" Yes, maybe it is a little unusual. But that's okay. Do it anyway. Suspend judgment and see what happens. To help you draft your letter, here's a really thoughtful one that Ashley wrote to her body to use as a model.

Dear Body of Mine,

For years, I've done nothing but criticize you. I can't believe the inconsiderate and unkind things I've said about you. I've really been thoughtless and disrespectful. I am so sorry! This is an apology I've owed you for a long time.

We've had some great times together and you've done a lot for me. Still, I never gave you the credit you really deserve. If it weren't for you, I wouldn't have been on my high school swim team or won that gymnastics award. I wouldn't have had so much fun at all the dances I've gone to or been able to take all those wonderful walks along the beach. And, oh yes, I wouldn't have been able to enjoy my first kiss! You've also managed to get me terrific compliments. People often say how warm your smile is and how nice you look in a new outfit.

Rather than see your assets and appreciate all you've done for me, I dwelled on how much you weigh. I know it's not fair for me to eat burritos, cheesecake, ice cream, and the other stuff, and then to blame you for gaining a few pounds. I've also said some pretty nasty things to you sometimes just because your hair isn't the way I want it to be at the moment.

Body of Mine, the truth is you're not so fat. I'm just scared you'll get fat, so I exaggerate sometimes. And I do like your hair. I expect too much perfection of you. Sorry! I hope you'll forgive me and we can have a better relationship from now on. I promise to be kinder to you. See you soon in the mirror!

With love and regrets, Ashley

Now it's your turn to write a letter to your body-partner.

Helpsheet for Change: Writing Wrongs

Dear Body of Mine,

_____

_____

_____

_____

_____

_____

_____

_____

_____

_____

_____

_____

_____

_____

_____

_____

_____

_____

Achieving and Pleasing with Positive Physical Activities

Bodies are much more than what they look like; they are instruments of action and sensation. People with a negative body image often neglect taking satisfaction from their bodies in ways that have nothing to do with appearance. Preoccupied with loathing, hiding, and repairing their looks, they also fail to find opportunities to enjoy their appearance. As stated above, Affirmative Actions are intended to improve your relationship with your body by doing special things to foster positive body image thoughts and feelings. These Affirmative Action opportunities fall into three categories of bodily experience: (1) physical health and fitness (i.e., feeling physically competent or healthy), (2) sensate experiences (i.e., your awareness of bodily sensations), and (3) physical appearance.

Within each of these categories, there are two psychological experiences that enhance your relationship with your body—mastery and pleasure. *Mastery* produces gratifying feelings of accomplishment from reaching a set goal. For example, setting and achieving the goal of running two miles or swimming ten laps can provide a satisfying sense of mastery. *Pleasure* simply means having fun. It doesn't require reaching a goal, only enjoying an activity because it inherently feels good. For instance, getting a massage or relaxing in a hot tub brings about calming, soothing sensations. Some activities furnish both mastery and pleasure. For example, aerobic dance involves mastering new moves and achieving improved fitness and also provides a pleasing, invigorating sense of bodily freedom.

Self-Discovery Helpsheet: Survey of Positive Physical Activities

For each activity below, rate how often you engaged in the activity during the past year. Then rate how much mastery you experienced and how much pleasure you felt. If you did not engage in the activity, rate the mastery and pleasure you would expect to feel.

Frequency during the past year:
0 = I never did this.
1 = I did this once or only a few times.
2 = I did this fairly often.
3 = I did this often.

The experience of **Mastery** refers to your sense of accomplishment or achievement felt when engaging in the activity.
0 = None
1 = Slight
2 = Moderate
3 = A lot

The experience of **Pleasure** refers to feeling enjoyment or having fun when engaging in the activity.
0 = None
1 = Slight
2 = Moderate
3 = A lot

Frequency	Mastery	Pleasure	Health and Fitness Activities
_____	_____	_____	1. Taking a long or brisk walk, jogging, or running
_____	_____	_____	2. Water recreation (swimming, scuba, snorkeling, waterskiing, surfing, windsurfing)
_____	_____	_____	3. Boating recreation (sailing, canoeing, kayaking, rowing, or rafting)
_____	_____	_____	4. Playing a team sport (baseball, softball, football, etc.)
_____	_____	_____	5. Roller-skating, roller-blading, skate-boarding, or ice-skating
_____	_____	_____	6. Playing tennis, racquetball, or squash
_____	_____	_____	7. Playing golf
_____	_____	_____	8. Working out on exercise machines or lifting weights
_____	_____	_____	9. Downhill skiing or cross-country skiing
_____	_____	_____	10. Hiking or rock climbing
_____	_____	_____	11. Indoor recreation (billiards, table tennis, bowling)
_____	_____	_____	12. Playing lawn sports (badminton, croquet, etc.)
_____	_____	_____	13. Horseback riding
_____	_____	_____	14. Bicycle riding
_____	_____	_____	15. Aerobic dance exercise
_____	_____	_____	16. Doing gymnastics or exercising on a trampoline
_____	_____	_____	17. Doing calisthenics (push-ups, sit-ups, etc.)
_____	_____	_____	18. Doing yoga
_____	_____	_____	19. Doing heavy outdoor work, lawn work, or gardening
_____	_____	_____	20. Individual dancing (ballet, expressive, etc.)
_____	_____	_____	21. Social dancing

Frequency	Mastery	Pleasure	Sensate Activites
_____	_____	_____	22. Getting a foot massage, back rub, or body massage
_____	_____	_____	23. Giving a body massage
_____	_____	_____	24. Having a scalp massage
_____	_____	_____	25. Having a manicure or pedicure
_____	_____	_____	26. Brushing your hair in a soothing manner
_____	_____	_____	27. Soaking in a hot tub
_____	_____	_____	28. Taking a relaxing shower or bath
_____	_____	_____	29. Sunbathing
_____	_____	_____	30. Having sexual relations
_____	_____	_____	31. Masturbating
_____	_____	_____	32. Rubbing your own body with lotion

Appearance-Oriented Activites

Frequency	Mastery	Pleasure	
_____	_____	_____	33. Getting a facial
_____	_____	_____	34. Getting a cosmetic makeover
_____	_____	_____	35. Wearing new or colorful clothes
_____	_____	_____	36. Wearing fashionable or formal clothes
_____	_____	_____	37. Wearing favorite casual clothes
_____	_____	_____	38. Wearing your hair in a different style
_____	_____	_____	39. Putting on makeup
_____	_____	_____	40. Wearing favorite jewelry
_____	_____	_____	41. Wearing cologne or perfume
_____	_____	_____	42. Brushing or whitening your teeth

Feel free to add other activities to the list!

Frequency	Mastery	Pleasure	Health and Fitness Activities
_____	_____	_____	_____
_____	_____	_____	_____
			Other Sensate Activities
_____	_____	_____	_____
_____	_____	_____	_____
			Other Appearance-Oriented Activities
_____	_____	_____	_____
_____	_____	_____	_____

Your Scores (see the text below to learn how to score your survey.)

Health and Fitness Activities: _____

Sensate Activites: _____

Appearance-Oriented Activities: _____

The following Self-Discovery Helpsheet lists possible sources of physical mastery and pleasure. Answer the survey questions to begin discovering potential ways to act affirmatively toward developing a more balanced, fulfilling relationship with your body.

Next, review your answers to the survey so that you can obtain your Positive Physical Activities scores. Here's how to do it:

- Regardless of how often you engaged in the activities, circle those that you rated as 2 or 3 on either pleasure or mastery.

- Classify the circled activities as relating either to health and fitness, sensate experiences, or physical appearance. Beside each, write *H* for health and fitness, *S* for sensate experiences, or *A* for appearance. If you find that some fall into more than one category, you may mark them more than once, but think about which category the activity fits best. Many activities have the potential to create different experiences for different people. For example, although some people would regard "getting a facial" as an appearance activity, others might regard it as sensate because of the tactile pleasure enjoyed during the process. Similarly, an activity like lifting weights can cover lots of experiential ground—enhancing feelings about appearance, promoting an awareness of being strong or fit, or evoking certain bodily sensations during the workout.

- Count the number of circled activities in each category. Omit any that aren't feasible to do within the next month. For example, don't count "sexual relations" if you're not in a sexual relationship. Forget about "rock climbing" if your arm is in a cast. For activities that relate to multiple categories, only count them in one primary category. Enter these scores at the bottom of the Self-Discovery Helpsheet. How many Health and Fitness Activities did you circle? How many Sensate Activities? And how many Appearance-Oriented Activities?

- Choose at least four activities from each of the three categories. If you have fewer than four, here are some ideas for coming up with more: Look for circled items that you can break down into more specific activities. For example, "playing team sports" lists multiple sports, so choose the ones you do. "Wearing favorite casual clothes" could be split into "wearing my favorite jeans" and "wearing my red bow tie." If there are activities that you initially placed in multiple categories but counted only in one primary category, reassign a few to a secondary category that needs more activities. Finally, to expand the list, ask yourself, "What have I done or considered doing that could lead me to feel physical mastery or pleasure?"

- Write down these twelve activities (or more!) on the following Helpsheet for Change. Soon you will use your chosen activities to build a better relationship with your body.

The next three sections of this chapter focus on the ways that you will use these activities for Affirmative Actions. By committing some of your quality time to these experiences, your relationship with your body has a very good chance to experience positive change.

Having Good Times with Health and Fitness Activities

Affirmative Actions for health and fitness nurture your experiences of physical competence and well-being. Routine exercise can benefit your body image, as well as your overall mental health. Compared to couch potatoes, whose only workouts are with the remote control for the television set, regular exercisers typically feel better about their fitness, their health, and also their appearance.

The most formidable obstacles to health and fitness activities pertain to motivation. Studies of people's motives for exercise reveal these four basic reasons: (1) to be more attractive or to lose weight; (2) to improve physical competence, fitness, and health; (3) to improve mood and manage stress; and (4) to meet, socialize with, and have fun with others.

Individuals with the first motive exercise to achieve a certain look—to look fit or slimmer or more muscular. Good health is incidental. Women are somewhat more likely than men to exercise primarily to manage their appearance and weight. Research has demonstrated that a negative body image is more prevalent among people who exercise for this reason. However, neither the mirror nor the scale measures your body's capabilities.

Helpsheet for Change: My Positive Physical Activities

Based on the results of your Survey of Positive Physical Activities, fill in the following:

List at least four Health and Fitness Activities that you will carry out:

1. _____
2. _____
3. _____
4. _____
5. _____
6. _____
7. _____

List at least four Sensate Activities that you will carry out:

1. _____
2. _____
3. _____
4. _____
5. _____
6. _____
7. _____

List at least four Appearance-Oriented Activities that you will carry out:

1. _____
2. _____
3. _____
4. _____
5. _____
6. _____
7. _____

Physical exercise is most psychologically rewarding when done for the right reasons. Becoming physically competent and fit is certainly a good reason. Physical competence and fitness reflect what your body can do—its athletic abilities, flexibility, coordination, strength, stamina, and endurance. This mastery component of exercise represents the second motivation listed above. This is certainly a healthy reason to exercise, unless taken to the extreme.

Compulsive exercisers' pursuit of physical mastery can become dangerously consuming, or even addictive, as they push themselves harder and harder to achieve ever-more rigorous feats of physical mastery. Driven to achieve perfect control over their bodies, ultimately they come to feel that their bodies control them. Illness, injury, and other interferences with exercise are exasperating and barely tolerated. They exercise more but with less enjoyment. By contrast, regular physical activity done in sensible moderation can benefit your emotional life and your body image. As for the other motives, exercise also can be a pleasurable way to socialize with others and it is an effective tool for managing stress.

One scholarly summary of research pointed to the positive effects of physical activity training on body image (Martin and Lichtenberger 2002). Moreover, these body image benefits don't necessarily require substantial improvements in fitness per se; nor do they require reductions in weight. For example, in 1994, psychologists at the University of South Florida (Fisher and Thompson) discovered that a program of aerobic activity and weight training fostered body image improvements. In 1995, Sherri Hensley-Crosson and I evaluated the effects of regular participation in an aerobic dance class. Not only did the exercisers enhance their cardiovascular fitness, they also developed a more satisfying body image than did their sedentary peers. In 2001, Pamela Williams and I investigated the effects of circuit weight training. When compared with a control group, those who did weight training had greater body image satisfaction, less physical self-consciousness, and improved feelings of physical competence. All of these studies showed body image improvements after several weeks.

To get more out of exercise, you should shift your attention away from issues of appearance or weight control and focus more on the satisfying experiences of physical mastery and pleasure. Learn how exercise can help you improve mood, manage stress, and enjoy the company of others. One excellent reason to be physically active is that you can have such good times working out with others.

This week, set aside time for one or two of the Health and Fitness Activities you selected. I'm not asking you to run a marathon or to start training for the Olympics. Of course, before embarking on an exercise program, especially if you've been inactive for a while or have any health problems, consult your physician about your plans.

Don't be so demanding or judgmental of your physical competence that you take all the fun out of exercise. As a Nike slogan says, "Just Do It!" While you engage in these activities, monitor your feelings of mastery and pleasure. On the Helpsheet that follows, rate your experiences. Each week, do just one or two of these activities, including the new ones, and record your experiences.

Having Good Times with Sensate Activities

Your body has millions of highly specialized cells that enable you to experience it and the world around you. You can take in the visual beauty of a colorful sunset or a baby's smile. You can sense the essence of fragrant flowers. You can savor your favorite flavor. You can experience the symphonic sounds of an orchestra or the melody of a distant songbird. You can feel your body move rhythmically to music.

Helpsheet for Change: My Positive Health and Fitness Activities

Ratings are 0 = None; 1 = Slight;   2 = Moderate;   3 = A lot.

Date	Health and Fitness Activity	Mastery	Pleasure

Helpsheet for Change: My Positive Sensate Activities

Ratings are 0 = None; 1 = Slight;   2 = Moderate;   3 = A lot.

Date	Sensate Activity	Pleasure
_____	_____	_____
_____	_____	_____
_____	_____	_____
_____	_____	_____
_____	_____	_____
_____	_____	_____
_____	_____	_____
_____	_____	_____
_____	_____	_____
_____	_____	_____
_____	_____	_____
_____	_____	_____
_____	_____	_____
_____	_____	_____
_____	_____	_____
_____	_____	_____
_____	_____	_____

You can feel your skin luxuriate in the sun's gentle warmth and the coolness of a soft breeze. You can be soothed by the caring touch of a loved one. If you're like most people, you take for granted such wonderful, sensate experiences. With all these riches that your body endows you, why dwell unappreciatively on what your body looks like?

Each week from now on, create opportunities to enjoy at least two of the Sensate Activities from your Positive Physical Activities Helpsheet. Schedule them and then carry them out. Mindfully immerse yourself in the pleasurable feelings that will arise. Let your sensate pleasure fill your consciousness. As enjoyable as these experiences may be, don't always schedule the same ones (like having sex!). Expand your sensory horizons to include activities such as bubble baths, head rubs (do it yourself if necessary), or body massages (with a little help from a friend). Use the Helpsheet to record the enjoyment you harvest each time. You need not rate mastery, of course. Sensate activities are treats of pleasure, not achievement.

Having Good Times with Appearance-Oriented Activities

In Steps 6 and 7, you began chiseling away at the various self-protective behaviors you use to manage your looks. You realize now that your Evasive Actions and Appearance-Preoccupied Rituals have undermined your body image. Many of these problematic patterns of behavior pertain to appearance management or grooming. But grooming doesn't have to create problems. It can enhance your feelings of mastery and pleasure. Whether your grooming affirms a positive body image or perpetuates a negative one depends on which type of groomer you are. There are three basic types:

1. The individual who Grooms to Hide and repeatedly checks and fixes her or his appearance is called the *Insatiable Groomer*. You will recognize this appearance-preoccupied pattern from Step 7. Primping, preening, fussing, and fretting are incessant. Satisfaction is fleeting.

2. A second pattern also seldom brings good times. *Gloomy Groomers* have given up on their looks. They mostly neglect their appearance, believing either that nothing could ever improve their looks or that they lack the ability to do so. Gloomy Groomers often fear doing anything to call attention to their body and invite self-consciousness. Therefore, they cling to a restricted range of "safe" looks. Some rationalize their pattern by thinking that grooming is somehow bad—self-absorbed or provocative.

    Consider Norma, who's worn the same aqua eye shadow, pink lipstick, and thick black mascara for about twenty years. She's pulled her hair into a ponytail for nearly as long. She always wears loose-fitting, ankle-length dresses, usually of solid black or dark gray. Norma "doesn't care for" her appearance. She's unwilling to attempt even simple grooming changes that would allow her to enjoy her looks more. To her, enjoying her looks would seem vain. Besides, she hasn't a clue of what she would do.

3. The first two types of grooming are clearly self-defeating. Insatiable Groomers stir up trouble. Gloomy Groomers want to leave bad enough alone. Both types have an inflexible relationship with their body's appearance. The third type of groomer has the best attitude. This *Flexible Groomer* is neither preoccupied with compulsive grooming nor neglectful of appearance. The Flexible Groomer has adaptively discovered a happy medium between unhappy extremes. My

Helpsheet for Change: My Positive Appearance-Oriented Activities

Ratings are 0 = None; 1 = Slight;   2 = Moderate;   3 = A lot.

Date	Appearance-Oriented Activity	Mastery	Pleasure

own research findings confirm the advantages of being a Flexible Groomer. For example, we found that women who are versatile in their use of facial makeup feel more in control socially than women who are rigid in their use of cosmetics (Cash, Rissi, and Chapman 1985). Further, women who always wear lots of makeup, no matter what situation they're in, underestimate their unadorned attractiveness (Cash et al. 1989). Their makeup is more a mask of self-imposed concealment than an optional and enjoyable adornment. Flexible grooming offers you choices and the affirming experience that you are acceptable with a variety of looks. It provides opportunities for pleasure and playfulness.

As a Flexible Groomer, Kristin's basic goal is to enhance her appearance in ways that express her individuality. She uses cosmetics in moderation, and she isn't reluctant to explore a new look from time to time. When selecting clothing colors and styles, Kristin wears what delights *her* eye—rather than conforming to the dictates of fashion or what best camouflages the thighs she's not so fond of. About once a year, she changes her hairstyle, simply because she experiences this as a refreshing change. Kristin doesn't depend on other people's compliments to enjoy her appearance. In fact, only a few friends know where her beloved butterfly tattoo is located. She doesn't aspire to be a flawless beauty; neither does she try to neutralize her looks. A Flexible Groomer like Kristin isn't afraid to look less than perfect or afraid to experiment.

Becoming a Flexible Groomer is possible through two parallel paths of action: First, keep using the lessons from Steps 6 and 7 to lessen your self-defensive grooming. Keep on Facing It and Erasing It! Second, carry out Affirmative Actions that provide positive appearance-oriented experiences. Learn to use the mood-altering tools of adornment—like clothing styles, fabrics, colors, cosmetics, hairstyles, jewelry, and fragrances—to enjoy your appearance. Don't work at it! Play at it! Flexible Grooming is fun.

Deriving enjoyment from your grooming activities doesn't mean you are a vain person. It just means you accept the body that's yours. What could be bad about that? Creating mastery experiences might involve figuring out how to put your clothes together to achieve a certain style you like and always thought you could never even attempt. It might involve learning how to apply makeup more effectively or how to do your hair in an easier-to-manage style. Be mindful of your motives, though. Mastery at concealing "defects" or at emulating a movie star is not healthy mastery.

Examine the Appearance-Oriented Activities that you listed on your Positive Physical Activities Helpsheet. Carry out a couple of these activities each week. Remember to record your experiences on the following Helpsheet. Enjoy the good times!

AFFIRMATIVE ACTIONS: AFFIRMING YOUR CHANGES

We began this chapter by recognizing that we each have an ongoing relationship with our body and that an unhappy body-self relationship requires positive experiences to promote positive change. You composed your Writing Wrongs letter of apology to your body and began to create rewarding experiences with it. In earlier Steps of this workbook, you've made genuine efforts to change the thoughts, feelings, and behaviors that interfere with your acceptance of your body.

Now it's time to reflect upon and appreciate the body image improvements that you have accomplished. This is a truly important Affirmative Action. I want you to take some quiet time, at least an hour, to contemplate this. Please be especially mindful and specific in your review of how your

Self-Discovery Helpsheet: How I've Improved My Body Image

_____

_____

_____

_____

_____

_____

_____

_____

_____

_____

_____

_____

_____

_____

_____

_____

_____

_____

_____

_____

experiences of your body have changed. How are you different in how you think, feel, and behave? This is not an invitation to think about what you haven't changed yet. In the Self-Discovery Helpsheet, write about each of the improvements, however big or small, that you've made in your relationship with your body. In your narrative, be sure to express how these improvements feel.

FINAL WORDS OF ENCOURAGEMENT

In our lives, our personal views of reality often hold us back, preventing us from becoming everything we can be. In the popular movie *Forrest Gump*, Forrest didn't understand that he wasn't supposed to be able to do all the things he imagined he could do. So he lived his dreams in accordance with what his mama taught him—that "life is like a box of chocolates. You never know what you're gonna get." She also taught him that "you have to do the best with what God gave you." So, despite his limitations and the challenges that life brought to him, he happily lived all of his aspirations. Just as Forrest created a successful life for himself, creating a positive relationship with your body is ultimately up to you.

What new Affirmative Actions can you dream up that would enhance your body image? Sorry, no suggestions from me on this one. Just be aware of your intuitive insights about what would be helpful to you. Challenge your creativity and put your innovative ideas into action. Be forever mindful of the good times that you have with your body.

In the following Afterword of your *Body Image Workbook*, I will share important tips to help you preserve the gains you've achieved and for handling any unforeseen challenges that may arise in the months and years ahead. So please keep reading!

From This Day Forward: Preserving Your Positive Body Image for Life

Can you believe it? You've completed the final step of your program for an improved, more accepting and satisfying body image. In saying farewell, however, I want to leave you with some thoughts about faring well in your body image future. How can you progress even further and preserve your positive changes?

HOW FAR HAVE YOU COME?

At the closing of Step 8, you summarized your experiences of body image improvement. You can also take stock of your body image "earnings" by using the body image self-tests from Step 1. Just go back and retake these self-tests. Score them and plot your "After" profile alongside your earlier "Before" profile. People are often pleasantly surprised when they compare their Before and After scores. Because individuals become accustomed to their positive changes fairly quickly, their memories of past problems fade and often they don't realize how much they've actually improved.

Rediscovering Your Needs, Resetting Your Goals

Of course, you may notice that some of your test scores that were originally in the Risky or Problem Zones didn't change much. Some improvements may just need more time. Some may need more deliberate and determined efforts from you. Moreover, independent of your Before and After score comparisons, you should be mindful of particular body image difficulties that linger. For example, there may be certain challenging situations, unhelpful assumptions or beliefs, troubling thoughts, or self-defeating behaviors that still present problems for you. Perhaps these are the very behaviors you haven't worked on yet or may still be working on.

Whatever the case, these should be on your to-do list for your continued mindful attention and efforts toward body image acceptance. To aid you in this task, I'll ask that you now complete the following Helpsheet for Change. On this Helpsheet you will identify areas for further change, and based on what you've learned in the workbook, you'll formulate some ideas and actions for getting there. In addition to reviewing your Before and After self-test results, return to the Helpsheet in Step 1 entitled My Needs for Change. What goals did you list then that haven't been realized as fully as you would like?

TROUBLESHOOTING

Although you cannot foresee every body image difficulty on the horizon, many problems can be anticipated. A forward-looking solution makes strength available by using the power of prevention. Take a little time to constructively look for trouble. What events and situations still evoke your negative body image emotions? What do these troublesome triggers have in common? For example, do they involve reactions of certain people? Do they entail others seeing particular parts of your body? Are they situations that spotlight your weight or body shape? Do they pertain to how your clothes look?

Whenever you expect to enter one of your "risky situations," don't start contemplating how to avoid it. That's the Beauty-Bound Distortion that leads to Evasive Actions. Relying on skills you've developed in this program, here are two ways to ready and steady yourself:

- The first strategy is to apply what you've learned in Steps 3 and 6. Create a Ladder of Success that breaks down the situation into elements that are progressively more difficult for you. Then, practice accepting and neutralizing your anticipated discomfort with mindfulness and Body-and-Mind Relaxation while visualizing these elements or events one at a time.

- The second strategy uses what you learned in Step 6. You'll PACE yourself. Prepare for the anticipated situation. Imagine being in the situation. Mentally rehearse how you want to deal with the worst-case scenario. Picture yourself handling it effectively. Act on your plan for confronting the situation. Cope as planned. Your New Inner Voice can support you through this tough time and will help to keep your Private Body Talk from becoming overloaded with mental mistakes. Stop, Look, and Listen! Your goal is simply to survive the situation, not to feel totally wonderful. Enjoy the fact that you stood up to adversity. Reward your courage.

Helpsheet for Change: My Needs and Plans
for Continued Improvements

Challenging situations:

_____

_____

My plans for improvement:

_____

_____

Unhelpful assumptions or beliefs:

_____

_____

My plans for improvement:

_____

_____

Troubling thoughts:

_____

_____

My plans for improvement:

_____

_____

Self-defeating behaviors:

_____

_____

My plans for improvement:

_____

_____

DEALING WITH PROVOCATIVE PEOPLE

For most individuals, many troublesome situations pertain to other people. There are at least three ways that people can provoke problems for your body image: (1) Their looks intimidate you. (2) They don't give you the body image strokes that you want. (3) They say things that set off the body image despair that you don't want. How can you deal with these people?

The "Beautiful" People

Some individuals "have no right to look so good." Their mere presence "makes" you feel unhappy with your appearance. Their looks remind you that you don't "measure up." You already know how to deal with these all-too-perfect-looking people. You stop committing the Unfair-to-Compare Distortion. Comparing yourself to them is unfair to both of you. Take them off the pedestal you've built for them. Just relate to them like regular folks, not like lofty kings or queens. Judge them based on what they say and do, instead of on how they look. If they're nice people, enjoy them. If they're jerks, move on!

The "Inattentive" People

Your spouse or romantic partner may sometimes be inattentive to your looks—not critical, but not complimentary either. "Gosh, you look so nice!" are words they seldom, if ever, express. As a result, you become insecure about what your partner privately thinks about your appearance. So, what can you do?

First, recognize your own mental mistakes. Are you committing the Mind Misreading Distortion and projecting your own negative thoughts into the other person's head? What factual proof do you have that the person has a negative opinion of your looks? What other explanations might exist to account for the person's inattentiveness? Consider these possibilities:

- Understand that some people never give compliments to anybody about anything. Obviously, the deficiency is theirs, not yours.

- Some people are totally "appearance blind"—oblivious to how others look and to how they themselves look. They don't comment on your appearance simply because it never crosses their mind to do so. "No news" isn't bad news. That's just the way these people are—apathetic about appearances.

- Another reason for their inattentiveness could be that they've "grown accustomed to your face" (and all other aspects of your looks). They take your appearance for granted, assets and all. If their silence and your uncertainty compel you to ask, "Do you find me attractive?" they usually reply, "Sure. You know I do." Familiarity doesn't breed contempt; it breeds complacency—about many things.

- One final reason that a particular person doesn't comment favorably on your appearance might be the "can of worms" explanation. A negative body image can lead some people to be vocally critical of their own looks and to engage in the Appearance-Preoccupied Ritual of excessive reassurance seeking. If the topic of your appearance is a well-worn subject, it's no wonder that this other person might be reluctant to reopen such a can of worms.

As you can see, there are abundant reasons that certain people may not compliment your looks. If you want strokes from these folks, your best chances are to go with the Golden Rule; so, do unto others. Behavioral scientists call this "the norm of reciprocity," which means that inattentiveness begets inattentiveness and that compliments beget compliments. Give sincere positive feedback when you notice that *they* look especially nice. If they reciprocate your compliment, accept it and tell them you appreciate it. If they don't, pay them compliments anyway. After all, being positive is its own reward. The best solution to this concern is not to depend on strokes from others in order to appreciate your looks. Punch your own ticket!

The "Insensitive" People

Do particular friends, loved ones, or acquaintances seem intent on making insensitive remarks that stir up your body image distress? Their comments can come in various forms:

- "Friendly" teasing: "You know I only kid you about your 'fuzzy' hair because we're good friends. If I didn't like you, I wouldn't kid you that way!"

- "Caring" concerns: "It's because I care about you that I can be honest about how terrible you look in shorts."

- "Helpful" advice: "I don't mean to hassle you about how chunky you've become. I'm just worried about your health. I only want what's best for you."

Short of buying them all a one-way airfare to a faraway place, how can you handle such insensitive people? Before I tell you, I want to alert you to recognize three common but definitely unproductive approaches: With the *passive*, or *unassertive*, approach, you don't want to "cause trouble" so you hide your hurt or annoyance and quietly sustain the insults—maybe even believing you deserve them. With an *aggressive* approach, you blow your cool and retaliate with hostile threats or insults. In the *passive-aggressive*, or *indirect*, approach, you sulk or become cranky or oppositional without ever telling the offender why you're acting this way.

The best way to deal with insensitive people is to take a rational, *assertive* course of action. Assertiveness is made easier if you better understand the other person, which can help to neutralize his or her unwelcome words. Ask yourself, "Where could this person be coming from?" Perhaps these people truly are trying to be friendly, or caring, or helpful. On the other hand, maybe they act insensitively because of their own body image insecurities. For example, parents who struggle with their own weight may shift their weight-watching burden onto their children. So they pass their misery along by nagging, "Why don't you go on a diet?" or "At your weight, you shouldn't be eating pie."

There are other plausible motives for insensitivity. Jealous partners or friends may worry that if you look too good, you'll have opportunities for other relationships. Their jabs at your appearance may be unconscious "controlling" efforts to diminish your self-confidence and prevent the possibility of losing you. Furthermore, did you ever stop to consider that critical people may be envious of you or your looks? You may be the focus of their own Unfair-to-Compare Distortions, and your appearance may cause them to feel unattractive. Or, perhaps because you intimidate them in some other way, they try to even the score by pointing out your physical imperfections.

After gaining some insight into possible motives for their insensitivity, make a plan for thoughtful assertive communication. Rational assertion has six sensible steps that you can remember easily with the acronym "RIGHTS":

1. **Review** the situation in advance. Identify what the problem is, how you feel about it, and how you're going to approach the offending person about it. Know exactly what you want to accomplish with assertive action. Because you want to be prepared and confident when you talk with the person, plan your words, write them down, and even practice them beforehand.

2. **Initiate** conversation with the person at a time and place that's mutually convenient. Don't just sit around and wait until you're offended again. It's preferable to talk without time pressures or distractions.

3. **Get specific** about the problem. Calmly and confidently tell the person the particular remarks or behaviors you find objectionable. Stay focused on the facts. Be descriptive without being accusatory. For instance, you might say something like "Recently, you've often mentioned that you think I ought to lose weight. I want to talk with you about your comments and how I feel about them." Don't take the passive path, meekly mumbling, "I'm really sorry to bring this up. It's probably petty and I'm just being overly sensitive, but...." Don't exaggerate or use aggressive, inflammatory words either—for example, "You are always bitching at me about being fat!" Don't stray off course into other issues—like "I'm really fed up with your insults about my weight and your total lack of consideration of me. You've never really been in my corner when I needed you. Like last year when you...."

4. **How you feel** is an essential aspect of what you will communicate. Use "I" statements to express how the objectionable behavior feels to you. For instance, "When you make jokes about my being so short, I feel hurt." Casting blame about how the person "makes" you feel will put him or her on the defensive. Keep the focus on your feelings, without tossing in opinionated conclusions. The statement "I felt embarrassed when we were at the beach and you criticized how I looked in my swimsuit" properly expresses an emotion. The proclamation "I feel you are a rude and insensitive scoundrel who takes great pleasure in humiliating me" is an opinion. The person can toss aside your opinion with "You're wrong!" It's much harder to dismiss or ignore your feelings.

5. **Target the change** you want. Offer a specific solution by stating what it is you want from the other person. For example, "I'm asking that from now on you stop calling me 'Jelly Butt' in front of our children." That's more precisely targeted than "I wish you'd stop being so damned hateful."

6. **Secure an agreement** from the person. Mention the inherent advantages to each of you that cooperation with your request would bring. Propose a win-win solution: "If you stop asking me whether I've lost weight, I'll take less time getting dressed before we go out, and I know I'll be more fun to be with." To negotiate change, offer positive consequences: "If you promise to refrain from criticizing my appearance today, I'll give you a back rub tonight." Of course, sometimes serious sanctions are called for—when the unwanted behavior is long-standing or when the offender has been unresponsive to previous requests for change. Under these circumstances, you may need to stipulate punitive outcomes for noncompliance with your assertive request: "I do want you to know in advance that if you make your usual jokes about my hair loss tonight, I will leave the party without you." Of course, whatever consequences you propose, positive or negative, must be ones that you are committed to follow through on.

By following the six steps of rational assertiveness—your RIGHTS, you take charge of how insensitive people affect your body image. If following these steps doesn't work at first, refine it and try again. You have a right to assert yourself and be treated with respect! But don't expect miracles. Most people don't change overnight, and some won't change at all.

BEING MINDFUL OF STAGNATING ATTITUDES

There are two obstacles to continued growth: First, as just discussed, your neglecting to think ahead, anticipate challenges, and troubleshoot can leave you vulnerable to ambush by adversities. Second, certain self-defeating attitudes can cause progress to stagnate.

Do you have any of the following five stagnating attitudes that could impede your improvements?

- The "Now Is Forever" attitude is a nasty notion that goes something like this: "Now that I've completed this workbook and I like my looks better, I'll never have to work on my body image again." This is like the attitude of some of the students I've taught, who think, "Now that I've taken the final exam, I can forget everything I've learned." What you've learned in this program will continue to be useful only if you mindfully continue to use it.

- The "Good Things Never Last" attitude espouses the opposite extreme. For example, some people become apprehensive when good things happen—if they are promoted at work or if they find themselves falling in love. Because they now have something valuable to lose, they start to worry and search for signs that their job or their romance may not be secure. Their actions then slowly sabotage their success and happiness, and they conclude, "I knew it all along. Good things never last." But, it's actually the case that their attitude sets a self-fulfilling prophecy in motion. With mindful efforts, good things surely do last.

- The "My Best Isn't Good Enough" attitude is a form of self-blaming used to explain unattained changes or an episode of body image distress. Should you have a perfectly positive, problem-free body image now that you've completed this workbook? Absolutely not! Learning new skills well enough to make them a natural part of your life takes time and practice. Furthermore, perfection is a myth—an unreasonable standard to judge yourself against whether or not you've done your best. Improvement builds on itself and on sustained effort, which is good enough. Tough times mean tough times, and that's all they mean. They are not an ultimate proof of your abilities or your character.

- The "Some Things Will Never Change" attitude is similar to the notion that your best is never enough. Both attitudes can cause what psychologists call *learned helplessness*. This happens when people give up because they decide that they have no control over events. If you resolve that some facet of your body image is unalterable, then you'll throw up your hands and do nothing to change it. So, obviously, nothing will change. On the other hand, if you put your pessimism on hold, set your goal, and work toward it, change has a real chance. Have you ever achieved things you once believed you couldn't?

- The "Bad Is Good" attitude justifies and perpetuates your lack of body acceptance. The notion here is that hating your body is crucial to your making desired body changes. So you insist on body loathing to motivate you to lift weights or lose weight. Beating yourself up is more likely to undermine your efforts to change your body in satisfying ways.

METAMORPHOSES

One thing that never changes is the fact that things will always change. Your body certainly has changed during your life, and it will continue to change. Some years ago, I went to my twenty-fifth high-school reunion. Many of us hadn't seen one another since graduation. Our reacquainting conversations often touched on how our current looks matched our recollections of each other, aided by circulating copies of our yellowed yearbook. "Wow, you look just the same!" was typically reserved for average- or better-looking classmates. "You look terrific; you really do!" was seemingly remarked to those whose attractiveness had improved over time. "So how have you been?" may have been the socially sensitive equivalent of "the aging process hasn't been too kind to you, has it?"

The former basketball team captain and hottie to most girls in the class was now a paraplegic, his body forever altered in the Vietnam War. The prettiest cheerleader, whose body had been ravaged by a potentially deadly disease, felt obliged to explain her appearance repeatedly during the course of the reunion. More than a few of the guys had substantial scalp to show for the quarter century that had passed. "Hair today, gone tomorrow," was a favorite quip. And then there was the woman with gray hair who warned us not to call her "Grandma." Classmates who'd added inches to their love handles groaned about how they had "grown" over the years. Some women displayed photos taken during pregnancy and sought reassurances that they were no longer "as big as a beached whale." Some smooth faces had weathered with a few wrinkles. And speaking of faces, where was Larry? We wondered if his cystic acne, about which he'd been so terribly teased, had scarred his life.

Time truly transforms everyone—psychologically and physically. With good nutrition, proper exercise, and other healthful practices, we can exert some control over the extent and rate of unwanted physical changes. But we can never look like kids again. This reality, however, doesn't seem to stop many of us from trying. We search for and buy fountain-of-youth products. We chase the promises of "take it off fast and forever" diets. We hire cosmetic surgeons to erase time with a scalpel, laser, or needle. What would happen if we devoted half of the effort we invest in trying to turn back the clock or have the perfect body to physical self-acceptance? The answer is profoundly simple: We would live happier lives.

FINAL WORDS OF ENCOURAGEMENT

The sum total of everything you've learned in *The Body Image Workbook* constitutes a new lifestyle and relationship between you and your body. This relationship will continue to grow and provide you with gratification just so long as you stay mindfully active in your efforts. There will be times you'll want to reread parts of this workbook as fuel for more thought and further action. Your personal Body Image Diary remains a valuable way for you to communicate with yourself about your troubles and to plan your triumphs. Once in a while, reread your journal of experiences to remind yourself of just how far you've come.

In the introduction to the workbook, I began by saying that the human condition is inherently one of embodiment. Indeed, in the wise words of the Greek philosopher Plato, "We are bound to our bodies like an oyster is to its shell." Yes, this is true; but we are not bound to be unhappy with our bodies. We can all come to live lives in which we accept the body we live in and the experiences that our body brings. I extend my heartfelt wishes to you for a mindful and satisfying life of body acceptance.

Recommended Resources for Readers, Researchers, and Therapists

Body image issues are very troublesome for a great many people. Fortunately, many individuals are able to work through their problems on their own with the aid of certain books, CDs, and tapes. The following resources are recommended to those readers who feel that they can handle their issues in an independent manner. Readers who feel that their body image problems are too difficult to resolve in this way and that they would benefit from professional guidance and counseling should consult the section below on how to find a practitioner. The lists below also include resources that are helpful for researchers and therapists.

BODY IMAGE RESOURCES

Consider reading the following works to learn more about body image—its development and assessment, and the prevention and treatment of body image difficulties and disorders. These are also valuable volumes for researchers and clinicians.

Books

Cash, T. F., and T. Pruzinsky (eds.). 2002. *Body Image: A Handbook of Theory, Research, and Clinical Practice*. New York: Guilford Press.

Castle, D. J., and K. A. Phillips (eds.). 2002. *Disorders of Body Image*. Philadelphia: Wrightson Biomedical Publishing.

Grogan, S. 2007. *Body Image: Understanding Body Dissatisfaction in Men, Women, and Children*. London: Psychology Press.

Partridge, J. 2006. *Changing Faces: The Challenge of Facial Disfigurement* 5th ed. London: Changing Faces.

Rumsey, N., and D. Harcourt. 2005. *The Psychology of Appearance.* Berkshire, England: Open University Press.

Sarwer, D. B., T. Pruzinsky, T. F. Cash, R. M. Goldwyn, J. A. Persing, and L. A. Whitaker (eds.). 2006. *Psychological Aspects of Reconstructive and Cosmetic Plastic Surgery: Clinical, Empirical, and Ethical Perspectives.* Philadelphia: Lippincott, Williams & Wilkins.

Thompson, J. K. (ed.). 2004. *Handbook of Eating Disorders and Obesity.* Hoboken, NJ: Wiley.

Thompson, J. K., and G. Cafri (eds.). 2007. *The Muscular Ideal: Psychological, Social, and Medical Perspectives.* Washington, DC: American Psychological Association.

Thompson, J. K., L. J. Heinberg, M. Altabe, and S. Tantleff-Dunn. 1999. *Exacting Beauty: Theory, Assessment, and Treatment of Body Image Disturbance.* Washington, DC: American Psychological Association.

Thompson, J. K., and L. Smolak (eds.). 2001. *Body Image, Eating Disorders, and Obesity in Youth: Assessment, Prevention, and Treatment.* Washington, DC: American Psychological Association.

For those readers who are particularly science-minded, take a look at *Body Image: An International Journal of Research* (T. F. Cash, editor-in-chief), published quarterly by Elsevier and accessible by ScienceDirect subscribers (www.sciencedirect.com). You can also visit the journal's website: www.elsevier.com/locate/bodyimage.

Body Image Measures for Researchers

Most of the books listed above include chapters that identify assessments of various aspects of body image functioning. Moreover, scientists who need validated body image assessments for their research may wish to consult these websites:

- www.body-images.com (website of T. F. Cash)

- www.bodyimagedisturbance.org (website of J. K. Thompson)

FINDING PRACTITIONERS

To find practitioners, the following two websites are particularly useful. Additional websites are listed below for specific problem areas.

- The Academy of Cognitive Therapy lists practitioners at www.academyofct.org.

- The Association of Behavioral and Cognitive Therapies lists practitioners at www.abct.org.

EATING DISORDER RESOURCES

Over the past several decades, eating disorders of every kind have become widespread throughout the United States. Every day brings new, alarming statistics about the prevalence of anorexia and bulimia among teenagers and young adults; the "epidemic" of obesity among children as well as adults; and the latest, possibly dangerous, fad diet that has caught the attention of that part of the population always seeking an new way to take off those unwanted ten, twenty, or fifty pounds. The following resources are recommended for readers with eating disorders (or early signs of eating disorders) who are looking for ways to cope with and overcome their problems with eating.

Books

Fairburn, C. G. 1995. *Overcoming Binge Eating*. New York: Guilford Press.

Heffner, M., G. H. Eifert, and K. Wilson. 2004. *The Anorexia Workbook: How to Accept Yourself, Heal Your Suffering, and Reclaim Your Life*. Oakland, CA: New Harbinger Publications.

Kalodner, C. R. 2003. *Too Fat or Too Thin? A Reference Guide to Eating Disorders*. New York: Guilford Press.

Lock, J., D. le Grange, W. S. Agras, and C. Dare. 2001. *Treatment Manual for Anorexia Nervosa: A Family-Based Approach*. New York: Guilford Press. (This book is particularly recommended for practitioners.)

McCabe, R. E., T. L. McFarlane, and M. P. Olmstead. 2003. *The Overcoming Bulimia Workbook: Your Comprehensive Step-by-Step Guide to Recovery*. Oakland, CA: New Harbinger Publications.

Websites

These sites offer listings of therapists and treatment facilities specializing in eating disorders, as well as links to professional eating disorder associations and conferences:

- An excellent website for publications (books, DVDs, newsletters, free articles) and other resources on eating disorders is www.bulimia.com (also www.gurze.com).

- Another highly informative resource is the Something Fishy website on eating disorders at www.something-fishy.com.

BODY DYSMORPHIC DISORDER RESOURCES

As discussed in the introduction to this book, body dysmorphic disorder (BDD) is a very distressing condition in which people develop a subjectively distorted perception of their looks, are intensely preoccupied with their appearance, engage in excessive appearance checking, and avoid situations where they might feel self-conscious. Here are excellent resources for individuals who have BDD and for the mental health professionals who help them.

Books

Claiborn, J., and C. Pedrick. 2002. *The BDD Workbook: Overcome Body Dysmorphic Disorder and End Body Image Obsessions.* Oakland, CA: New Harbinger Publications.

Phillips, K. A. 2005. *The Broken Mirror: Understanding and Treating Body Dysmorphic Disorder.* Rev. ed. New York: Oxford University Press.

Pope, H. G., Jr., K. A. Phillips, and R. Olivardia. 2000. *The Adonis Complex: The Secret Crisis of Male Body Obsession.* New York: Free Press.

Wilhelm, S. 2006. *Feeling Good about the Way You Look.* New York: Guilford Press.

Websites

Here is a partial list of websites from programs that specialize in the treatment of BDD and related disorders:

- BDD Central at www.bddcentral.com is a valuable website. In addition to educational information, it gives treatment referral resources.

- BDD Treatment Programme at the Priory Hospital North London, UK: www.veale.co.uk/bdd.html

- Bio-Behavioral Institute in Great Neck, New York: www.bio-behavioral.com/bdd.asp

- Body Dysmorphic Disorder Clinic and Research Unit at Massachusetts General Hospital and Harvard Medical School: www.massgeneral.org/bdd

- Body Image Program at Butler Hospital (Providence, Rhode Island): www.bodyimageprogram.com (or http://www.butler.org/body.cfm?id=123)

- Compulsive and Impulsive Disorders Program at Mount Sinai School of Medicine (New York, NY): www.mssm.edu/psychiatry/ciadp

MINDFULNESS AND ACCEPTANCE RESOURCES

As reflected in this workbook, mindfulness and acceptance approaches to personal growth and psychotherapy can be highly effective. A prominent pioneer of this approach, Jon Kabat-Zinn, has written several excellent and inspiring books, and he has produced three series of Mindfulness Meditation Practice Programs in audio CD or tape format. His website at www.jonkabat-zinn.com offers a wealth of information, including how to order the following resources.

Williams, J. M. G., J. D. Teasdale, Z. V. Segal, and J. Kabat-Zinn. 2007. *The Mindful Way through Depression: Freeing Yourself from Chronic Unhappiness*. New York: Guilford Press. Includes a guided meditation tape by J. Kabat-Zinn.

Kabat-Zinn, J. 2005. *Coming to Our Senses: Healing Ourselves and the World through Mindfulness*. New York: Hyperion.

Kabat-Zinn, J. 1994. *Wherever You Go There You Are: Mindfulness Meditation in Everyday Life*. New York: Hyperion.

Kabat-Zinn, J. 1990. *Full-Catastrophe Living: Using the Wisdom of Your Body and Mind to Face Stress, Pain, and Illness*. New York: Delacorte.

Mindfulness for Beginners (Sounds True 2006) audio CD series.

Guided Mindfulness Meditation (Sounds True 2005) audio CD series.

New Harbinger, the publisher of this workbook, has a number of informative resources on mindfulness and acceptance, titles listed below. Visit the publisher's website at www.newharbinger.com:

Alpers. S. 2003. *Eating Mindfully*. Oakland, CA: New Harbinger Publications.

Brantley, J. 2003. *Calming Your Anxious Mind*. Oakland, CA: New Harbinger Publications.

Brantley, J., and W. Millstine. 2005. *Five Good Minutes*. Oakland, CA: New Harbinger Publications.

Hayes, S., and S. Smith. 2005. *Get Out of Your Mind and Into Your Life*. Oakland, CA: New Harbinger Publications.

McKay, M., and C. Sutker. 2007. *Leave Your Mind Behind*. Oakland, CA: New Harbinger Publications.

McQuaid, J., and P. Carmona. 2004. *Peaceful Mind*. Oakland, CA: New Harbinger Publications.

Spradlin, S. 2003. *Don't Let Your Emotions Run Your Life*. Oakland, CA: New Harbinger Publications.

Thoughts for Therapists

The original edition of *The Body Image Workbook* has been used successfully by many professional therapists for helping their clients overcome distressing body image thoughts, feelings, and experiences. The workbook has been widely adopted in hospitals, clinics, and private practices as a body image module for treating eating disorders. For example, in her clinical practice, Dr. Stacey Nye used the workbook to conduct effective body image therapy groups for her clients with eating disorders (see Nye and Cash 2006). This workbook specifically, and cognitive behavioral body image more generally, have received strong empirical support in the treatment of body image difficulties and disorders (Hrabosky and Cash 2001; Jarry and Bernardi 2004; Jarry and Ip 2005). Therefore this workbook will be especially valuable to those committed to evidence-based practice. If you are a therapist or counselor and plan to use this program with your clients, allow me to offer the following recommendations.

The Body Image Workbook can be used in either individual or group formats by therapists trained in cognitive behavioral therapies. It can make your practice of body image therapy more systematic and efficient. Workbook assignments and Helpsheets offer clear guidance to promote change. In face-to-face sessions, you review the client's workbook entries and activities and provide the support and feedback the client needs.

The program is structured as eight discrete steps that cumulatively build the client's skills and integrate therapeutic techniques. However, your professional judgment should dictate your priorities in introducing and pacing the components of the program to fit the individual client's needs. You may wisely decide to focus more thoroughly on some steps than on others, based on the nature of the client's specific body image difficulties.

Facets of the workbook are valuable for addressing the body image difficulties that accompany a range of other presenting problems—social anxiety, depression, sexual dysfunctions, and basic self-esteem issues, for example. Of course, the program should never be the sole treatment for these clients. In clinical practice, your thorough assessment of each client's functioning and primary complaints is essential. You must have an accurate understanding of the functional significance of the client's body image in relation to other aspects of his or her psychosocial problems. However, you can effectively integrate this program with the proper treatments of these problems.

Of course, simply telling a client to Read this book won't be helpful. Good clinical care necessitates meaningfully integrating the workbook into the client's broader treatment plan and providing problem-solving guidance and support. Moreover, as one who believes strongly in science-based practice, I encourage you to collect data on your clients' targeted changes resulting from the therapeutic procedures that you use.

I sincerely hope that you will find *The Body Image Workbook* to be an efficient, effective, and valuable resource in your clinical practice or treatment program. Helping clients who struggle with a broad range of body image difficulties makes an significant contribution to the quality of their lives.

Bibliography

The following references are for explicitly or implicitly cited sources in this book, including pertinent citations potentially useful to readers.

American Psychiatric Association. 2000. *Diagnostic and Statistical Manual of Mental Disorders*. 4th ed. Text revision. Washington, DC: American Psychiatric Association.

American Society of Plastic Surgeons. 2007. *Report of the 2006 Statistics*. National Clearinghouse of Plastic Surgery Statistics. Report available from the ASPS website at www.plasticsurgery.org.

Annis, N. M., T. F. Cash, and J. I. Hrabosky. 2004. Body image and psychosocial differences among stable average-weight, currently overweight, and formerly overweight women: The role of stigmatizing experiences. *Body Image: An International Journal of Research* 1:155-167.

Baer, R. A. (ed.) 2006. *Mindfulness-Based Treatment Approaches: Clinician's Guide to Evidence Base and Applications*. New York: Academic Press.

Bandura, A. 1977. Self-efficacy: Toward a unifying theory of behavior change. *Psychological Review* 84:191-215.

Beck, A. T. 1976. *Cognitive Therapy and the Emotional Disorders*. New York: International Universities Press.

Bernstein, N. R. 1990. Objective bodily damage: Disfigurement and dignity. In *Body Images: Development, Deviance, and Change*, edited by T. F. Cash and T. Pruzinsky. New York: Guilford Press.

Britton, L., D. M. Martz, D. Bazzini, L. Curtin, and A. Leashomb. 2006. Fat talk and self-presentation of body image: Is there a social norm for women to self-degrade? *Body Image: An International Journal of Research* 3:247-254.

Brown, T. A., T. F. Cash, and P. J. Mikulka. 1990. Attitudinal body image assessment: Factor analysis of the Body-Self Relations Questionnaire. *Journal of Personality Assessment* 55:135-144.

Brownell, K. D., and J. Rodin. 1994. The dieting maelstrom: Is it possible and advisable to lose weight? *American Psychologist* 49:781-791.

Butters, J. W., and T. F. Cash. 1987. Cognitive-behavioral treatment of women's body-image dissatisfaction. *Journal of Consulting and Clinical Psychology* 55:889-897.

Cash, T. F. 1990. The psychology of physical appearance: Aesthetics, attributes, and images. In *Body Images: Development, Deviance, and Change*, edited by T. F. Cash and T. Pruzinsky. New York: Guilford Press.

———. 1991. *Body-Image Therapy: A Program for Self-Directed Change*. New York: Guilford Press.

———. 1993. Body-image attitudes among obese enrollees in a commercial weight-loss program. *Perceptual and Motor Skills* 77:1099-1103.

———. 1994a. Body image and weight changes in a multisite comprehensive very low-calorie diet program. *Behavior Therapy* 25:239-254.

———. 1994b. The Situational Inventory of Body-Image Dysphoria: Contextual assessment of a negative body image. *Behavior Therapist* 17:133-134.

———. 1995a. Developmental teasing about physical appearance: Retrospective descriptions and relationships with body image. *Personality and Social Behavior: An International Journal* 23:123-130.

———. 1995b. The psychosocial effects of adolescent facial acne: Its severity and management in a medically untreated sample. Technical report to the Neutrogena Corporation, Los Angeles, CA.

———. 1995c. *What Do You See When You Look in the Mirror? Helping Yourself to a Positive Body Image*. New York: Bantam Books.

———. 1996. Remembrance of things past: A scientific investigation of the vestigial psychological effects of adolescent acne in early adulthood. Technical report to the Neutrogena Corporation, Los Angeles, CA.

———. 1997. *The Body Image Workbook: An 8-Step Program for Learning to Like Your Looks*. Oakland, CA: New Harbinger Publications.

———. 1999. The psychosocial consequences of androgenetic alopecia: A review of the research literature. *British Journal of Dermatology* 141:398-405.

———. 2000a. Body image. In *The Encyclopedia of Psychology*, edited by A. Kazdin. Washington, D.C: American Psychological Association and Oxford University Press.

———. 2000b. The users' manual for the Multidimensional Body-Self Relations Questionnaire. Available from the author at www.body-images.com.

———. 2001. The psychology of hair loss and its implications for patient care. *Clinics in Dermatology* 19:161-166.

———. 2002a. A "negative body image": Evaluating epidemiological evidence. In *Body Image: A Handbook of Theory, Research, and Clinical Practice*, edited by T. F. Cash and T. Pruzinsky. New York: Guilford Press.

————. 2002b. Cognitive behavioral perspectives on body image. In *Body Image: A Handbook of Theory, Research, and Clinical Practice,* edited by T. F. Cash and T. Pruzinsky. New York: Guilford Press.

————. 2002c. The Situational Inventory of Body-Image Dysphoria: Psychometric evidence and development of a short form. *International Journal of Eating Disorders* 32:362-366.

————. 2002d. Women's body images. In *Handbook of Women's Sexual and Reproductive Health,* edited by G. Wingood and R. DiClemente. New York: Plenum Press.

————. 2004. Body image: Past, present, and future. *Body Image: An International Journal of Research* 1:1-5.

————. 2008. *Measures and manuals for the multidimensional assessment of body image.* Available from the author at www.body-images.com.

Cash, T. F., and J. W. Butters. 1986. *Cognitive-Behavioral Treatment of Body-Image Dissatisfaction: Manual of Procedures and Materials.* Norfolk, VA: Department of Psychology, Old Dominion University.

Cash, T. F., B. Counts, and C. E. Huffine. 1990. Current and vestigial effects of overweight among women: Fear of fat, attitudinal body image, and eating behaviors. *Journal of Psychopathology and Behavioral Assessment* 12:157-167.

Cash, T. F., K. Dawson, P. Davis, M. Bowen, and C. Galumbeck. 1989. The effects of cosmetics use on the physical attractiveness and body image of college women. *Journal of Social Psychology* 129:349-356.

Cash, T. F., and E. A. Deagle. 1997. The nature and extent of body-image disturbances in anorexia nervosa and bulimia nervosa: A meta-analysis. *International Journal of Eating Disorders* 22:107-125.

Cash, T. F., and E. C. Fleming. 2002a. Body image and social relations. In *Body Image: A Handbook of Theory, Research, and Clinical Practice,* edited by T. F. Cash and T. Pruzinsky. New York: Guilford Press.

————. 2002b. The impact of body-image experiences: Development of the Body Image Quality of Life Inventory. *International Journal of Eating Disorders* 31:455-460.

Cash, T. F., and K. M. Grasso. 2005. The norms and stability of new measures of the multidimensional body image construct. *Body Image: An International Journal of Research* 2:199-203.

Cash, T. F., and P. E. Henry. 1995. Women's body images: The results of a national survey in the U.S.A. *Sex Roles* 33:19-28.

Cash, T. F., and K. L. Hicks. 1990. Being fat versus thinking fat: Relationships with body image, eating behaviors, and well-being. *Cognitive Therapy and Research* 14:327-341.

Cash, T. F., and J. I. Hrabosky. 2003. The effects of psychoeducation and self-monitoring in a cognitive-behavioral program for body-image improvement. *Eating Disorders: A Journal of Treatment and Prevention* 11:255-270.

————. 2004. The treatment of body-image disturbances. In *Handbook of Eating Disorders and Obesity,* edited by K. Thompson. New York: Wiley.

Cash, T. F., and L. Jacobi. 1992. Looks aren't everything (to everybody): The strength of ideals of physical appearance. *Journal of Social Behavior and Personality* 7:621-630.

Cash, T. F., T. A. Jakatdar, and E. F. Williams. 2004. The Body Image Quality of Life Inventory: Further validation with college men and women. *Body Image: An International Journal of Research* 1:279-287.

Cash, T. F., and L. H. Janda. 1984. Eye of the beholder. *Psychology Today* 18:46-52.

Cash, T. F., and A. S. Labarge. 1996. Development of the Appearance Schemas Inventory: A new cognitive body-image assessment. *Cognitive Therapy and Research* 20:37-50.

Cash, T. F., and D. M. Lavallee. 1997. Cognitive-behavioral body-image therapy: Further evidence of the efficacy of a self-directed program. *Journal of Rational-Emotive and Cognitive-Behavior Therapy* 15:281-294.

Cash, T. F., R. J. Lewis, and P. Keeton. 1987. Development and validation of the Body-Image Automatic Thoughts Questionnaire. Paper presented at the annual convention of the Southeastern Psychological Association, Atlanta, GA.

Cash, T. F., C. L. Maikkula, and Y. Yamamiya. 2004. "Baring the body in the bedroom": Body image, sexual self-schemas, and sexual functioning among college women and men. *Electronic Journal of Human Sexuality* 7 (www.ejhs.org/volume7/bodyimage.html).

Cash, T. F, S. E. Melnyk, and J. I. Hrabosky. 2004. The assessment of body-image investment: An extensive revision of the Appearance Schemas Inventory. *International Journal of Eating Disorders* 35:305-316.

Cash, T. F., J. A. Morrow, J. I. Hrabosky, and A. A. Perry. 2004. How has body image changed? A cross-sectional study of college women and men from 1983 to 2001. *Journal of Consulting and Clinical Psychology* 72:1081-1089.

Cash, T. F., J. Muth, P. Williams, and L. Rieves. 1996. Assessments of body image: Measuring cognitive and behavioral components. Poster presented at the annual convention of the Association for Advancement of Behavior Therapy, New York.

Cash, T. F., P. Novy, and J. Grant. 1994. Why do women exercise?: Factor analysis and further validation of the Reasons for Exercise Inventory. *Perceptual and Motor Skills* 78:539-544.

Cash, T. F., K. A. Phillips, M. T. Santos, and J. I. Hrabosky. 2004. Measuring "negative body image": Validation of the Body Image Disturbance Questionnaire in a nonclinical population. *Body Image: An International Journal of Research* 1:363-372.

Cash, T. F., and T. Pruzinsky (eds.). 1990. *Body Images: Development, Deviance, and Change*. New York: Guilford Press.

———. 2002. *Body Image: A Handbook of Theory, Research, and Clinical Practice*. New York: Guilford Press.

Cash, T. F., J. Rissi, and R. Chapman. 1985. Not just another pretty face: Sex roles, locus of control, and cosmetics use. *Personality and Social Psychology Bulletin* 11:246-257.

Cash, T. F., R. E. Roy, and M. D. Strachan. 1997. How physical appearance affects relations among women: Implications for women's body images. Poster presented at the annual convention of the American Psychological Society, Washington, DC.

Cash, T. F., J. A. Rudiger, and E. F. Williams. 2008. Protective factors in positive body image development: A qualitative study. Manuscript submitted for publication.

Cash, T. F., M. T. Santos, and E. F. Williams. 2005. Coping with body-image threats and challenges: Validation of the Body Image Coping Strategies Inventory. *Journal of Psychosomatic Research* 58:191-199.

Cash, T. F., and M. D. Strachan. 2002. Cognitive behavioral approaches to changing body image. In *Body Image: A Handbook of Theory, Research, and Clinical Practice*, edited by T. F. Cash and T. Pruzinsky. New York: Guilford Press.

Cash, T. F., J. Theriault, and N. M. Annis. 2004. Body image in an interpersonal context: Adult attachment, fear of intimacy, and social anxiety. *Journal of Social and Clinical Psychology* 23:89-103.

Cash, T. F., B. A. Winstead, and L. H. Janda. 1986 The great American shape-up: Body image survey report. *Psychology Today* 20:30-37.

Castle, D. J., and K. A. Phillips (eds.) 2002. *Disorders of Body Image*. Philadelphia: Wrightson Biomedical Publishing.

Celio, A. A., M. F. Zabinski, and D. E. Wilfley. 2002. African American body images. In *Body Image: A Handbook of Theory, Research, and Clinical Practice*, edited by T. F. Cash and T. Pruzinsky. New York: Guilford Press.

Ciliska, D. 1990. *Beyond Dieting: Psychoeducational Interventions for Chronically Obese Women, a Nondieting Approach*. New York: Brunner/Mazel.

Claiborn, J., and C. Pedrick. 2002. *The BDD Workbook: Overcome Body Dysmorphic Disorder and End Body Image Obsessions*. Oakland, CA: New Harbinger Publications.

Davis, C. 2002. Body image and athleticism. In *Body Image: A Handbook of Theory, Research, and Clinical Practice*, edited by T. F. Cash and T. Pruzinsky. New York: Guilford Press.

Delinsky, S. S., and G. T. Wilson. 2006. Mirror exposure for the treatment of body image disturbance. *International Journal of Eating Disorders* 39:108-116.

Eagly, A. H., R. D. Ashmore, M. G. Makhijani, and L. C. Kennedy. 1991. What is beautiful is good, but...: A meta-analytic review of research on the physical attractiveness stereotype. *Psychological Bulletin* 110:226-235.

Fairburn, C. G. 1995. *Overcoming Binge Eating*. New York: Guilford Press.

Fairburn, C. G., and K. D. Brownell (eds.). 2002. *Eating Disorders and Obesity: A Comprehensive Handbook*. 2nd ed. New York: Guilford Press.

Fallon, A. E. 1990. Culture in the mirror: Sociocultural determinants of body image. In *Body Images: Development, Deviance, and Change*, edited by T. F. Cash and T. Pruzinsky. New York: Guilford Press.

Feingold, A. 1988. Matching for attractiveness in romantic partners and same-sex friends: A meta-analysis and theoretical critique. *Psychological Bulletin* 104:226-235.

———. 1992. Good-looking people are not what we think. *Psychological Bulletin* 111:304-341.

Feingold, A., and R. Mazzella. 1998. Gender differences in body image are increasing. *Psychological Science* 9:190-195.

Fisher, E., and J. K. Thompson. 1994. A comparative evaluation of cognitive-behavioral therapy (CBT) versus exercise therapy (ET) for the treatment of body image disturbance. *Behavior Modification* 18:171-185.

Flegal, K. M., M. D. Carroll, C. L. Ogden, et al. 2002. Prevalence and trends in obesity among U.S. adults. *Journal of the American Medical Association* 288:1723-1727.

Foreyt, J. P., and G. K. Goodrick. 1992. *Living Without Dieting*. Houston, TX: Harrison.

Foster, G. D., and P. E. Matz. 2002. Weight loss and changes in body image. In *Body Image: A Handbook of Theory, Research, and Clinical Practice*, edited by T. F. Cash and T. Pruzinsky. New York: Guilford Press.

Foster, G. D., and B. G. McGuckin. 2002. Nondieting approaches: Principles, practices, and evidence. In *Handbook of Obesity*, edited by T. A. Wadden and A. J. Stunkard. New York: Guilford Press.

Foster, G. D., T. A. Wadden, and R. A. Vogt. 1997. Body image before, during, and after weight loss treatment. *Health Psychology* 16:226-229.

Garner, D. M. 2002. Body image and anorexia nervosa. In *Body Image: A Handbook of Theory, Research, and Clinical Practice*, edited by T. F. Cash and T. Pruzinsky. New York: Guilford Press.

Germer, C. K., R. D. Siegel, and P. R. Fulton (eds.). 2005. *Mindfulness and Psychotherapy*. New York: Guilford Press.

Grant, J. R., and T. F. Cash. 1995. Cognitive-behavioral body-image therapy: Comparative efficacy of group and modest-contact treatments. *Behavior Therapy* 26:69-84.

Grasso, K. M., T. F. Cash, T. Yanover, and J. K. Thompson. 2007. An expressive writing intervention for body image: A randomized controlled trial. Poster presented at the annual convention of the Association for Behavioral and Cognitive Therapies, Philadelphia.

Grilo, C. M. 2002. Binge eating disorder. In *Eating Disorders and Obesity: A Comprehensive Handbook*, edited by C. G. Fairburn and K. D. Brownell. New York: Guilford Press.

Grogan, S. 2007. *Body Image: Understanding Body Dissatisfaction in Men, Women, and Children*. London: Psychology Press.

Hangen, J. D., and T. F. Cash. 1991. Body-image attitudes and sexual functioning in a college population. Poster presented at the annual convention of the Association for Advancement of Behavior Therapy, New York.

Hayes, S. C., V. M. Follette, and M. M. Linehan (eds.). 2004. *Mindfulness and Acceptance: Expanding the Cognitive-Behavioral Tradition*. New York: Guilford Press.

Hayes, S. C., and S. Smith. 2005. *Get Out of Your Mind and Into Your Life: The New Acceptance and Commitment Therapy*. Oakland, CA: New Harbinger Publications.

Heffner, M., G. H. Eifert, and K. Wilson. 2004. *The Anorexia Workbook: How to Accept Yourself, Heal Your Suffering, and Reclaim Your Life*. Oakland, CA: New Harbinger Publications.

Hensley-Crosson, S. L., and T. F. Cash. 1995. The effects of aerobic exercise on state and trait body image and physical fitness among college women. Poster presented at the annual convention of the Association for Advancement of Behavior Therapy, Washington, DC.

Hilbert, A., B. Tuschen-Caffier, and C. Vögele, C. 2002. Effects of prolonged and repeated body image exposure in binge-eating disorder. *Journal of Psychosomatic Research* 52:137-144.

Hill, J. O., V. Catenacci, and H. R. Wyatt 2005. Obesity: Overview of an epidemic. *Psychiatric Clinics of North America* 28:1-23.

Hrabosky, J. I., and T. F. Cash. 2007. Self-help treatment for body image disturbances. In *Self-Help Approaches for Obesity and Eating Disorders: Research and Practice*, edited by J. D. Latner and G. T. Wilson. New York: Guilford Press.

Jackson, L. A. 1992. *Physical Appearance and Gender: Sociobiological and Sociocultural Perspectives*. Albany: SUNY Press.

———. 2002. Physical attractiveness: A sociocultural perspective. In *Body Image: A Handbook of Theory, Research, and Clinical Practice*, edited by T. F. Cash and T. Pruzinsky. New York: Guilford Press.

Jacobi, L., and T. F. Cash. 1994. In pursuit of the perfect appearance: Discrepancies among self-ideal percepts of multiple physical attributes. *Journal of Applied Social Psychology* 24:379-396.

Jakatdar, T. A., T. F. Cash, and E. K. Engle. 2006. Body-image thought processes: The development and initial validation of the Assessment of Body-Image Cognitive Distortions. *Body Image: An International Journal of Research* 3:325-333.

Jarry, J. L., and K. Berardi. 2004. Characteristics and effectiveness of stand-alone body image treatments: A review of the empirical literature. *Body Image: An International Journal of Research* 1:319-333.

Jarry, J. L., and K. Ip. 2005. The effectiveness of stand-alone cognitive-behavioural therapy for body image: A meta-analysis. *Body Image: An International Journal of Research* 2:317-331.

Kabat-Zinn, J. 1990. *Full-Catastrophe Living: Using the Wisdom of Your Body and Mind to Face Stress, Pain, and Illness*. New York: Delacorte Press.

———. 1994. *Wherever You Go, There You Are: Mindfulness Meditation in Everyday Life*. New York: Hyperion.

———. 2005. *Coming to Our Senses: Healing Ourselves and the World Through Mindfulness*. New York: Hyperion.

Kalodner, C. R. 2003. *Too Fat or Too Thin? A Reference Guide to Eating Disorders*. New York: Guilford Press.

Kearney-Cooke, A. 2002. Familial influences on body image development. In *Body Image: A Handbook of Theory, Research, and Clinical Practice*, edited by T. F. Cash and T. Pruzinsky. New York: Guilford Press.

Key, A., C. L. George, D. Beattie, K. Stammers, H. Lacey, and G. Waller. 2002. Body image treatment within an inpatient program for anorexia nervosa: The role of mirror exposure in the desensitization process. *International Journal of Eating Disorders* 31:85-190.

Kleck, R. E., and A. Strenta. 1980. Perceptions of the impact of negatively valued physical characteristics on social interaction. *Journal of Personality and Social Psychology* 39:861-873.

Latner, J. D., and G. T. Wilson (eds.). 2007. *Self-Help Approaches for Obesity and Eating Disorders: Research and Practice*. New York: Guilford Press.

Lavallee, D. M., and T. F. Cash. 1997. The comparative efficacy of two self-help programs for a negative body image. Poster presented at the annual conference of the Association for Advancement of Behavior Therapy, Miami Beach, FL.

Lepore, S. J., and J. M. Smyth. 2002. *The Writing Cure: How Expressive Writing Promotes Health and Emotional Well-Being*. Washington, DC: American Psychological Association.

Levine, M. P., and L. Smolak. 2002. Body image development in adolescence. In *Body Image: A Handbook of Theory, Research, and Clinical Practice*, edited by T. F. Cash and T. Pruzinsky. New York: Guilford Press.

Lock, J., D. le Grange, W. S. Agras, and C. Dare. 2001. *Treatment Manual for Anorexia Nervosa: A Family-Based Approach*. New York: Guilford Press.

Markus, H. 1977. Self-schemata and processing information about the self. *Journal of Personality and Social Psychology* 35:63-78.

Markus, H., R. Hamill, and K. P. Sentis. 1987. Thinking fat: Self-schemas for body weight and the processing of weight-relevant information. *Journal of Applied Social Psychology* 17:50-71.

Marra, T. 2005. *Dialectical Behavior Therapy in Private Practice: A Practical and Comprehensive Guide*. Oakland, CA: New Harbinger Publications.

Martin, K. A., and C. M. Lichtenberger. 2002. Fitness enhancement and changes in body image. In *Body Image: A Handbook of Theory, Research, and Clinical Practice*, edited by T. F. Cash and T. Pruzinsky. New York: Guilford Press.

McCabe, R. E., T. L. McFarlane, and M. P. Olmstead. 2003. *The Overcoming Bulimia Workbook: Your Comprehensive Step-by-Step Guide to Recovery*. Oakland, CA: New Harbinger Publications.

McKinley, N. M. 2002. Feminist perspectives and objectified body consciousness. In *Body Image: A Handbook of Theory, Research, and Clinical Practice*, edited by T. F. Cash and T. Pruzinsky. New York: Guilford Press.

Melnyk, S. E., T. F. Cash, and L. H. Janda. 2004. Body image ups and downs: Prediction of intra-individual level and variability of women's daily body image experiences. *Body Image: An International Journal of Research* 1:225-235.

Morrison, M. A., T. G. Morrison, and C. L. Sager. 2004. Does body satisfaction differ between gay men and lesbian women and heterosexual men and women? A meta-analytic review. *Body Image: An International Journal of Research* 1:127-138.

Muth, J. L., and T. F. Cash. 1997. Body-image attitudes: What difference does gender make? *Journal of Applied Social Psychology* 27:1438-1452.

Nichter, M. 2000. *Fat Talk: What Girls and Their Parents Say about Dieting*. Cambridge, MA: Harvard University Press.

Noles, S. W., T. F. Cash, and B. A. Winstead. 1985. Body image, physical attractiveness, and depression. *Journal of Consulting and Clinical Psychology* 53:88-94.

Nye, S., and T. F. Cash. 2006. Outcomes of manualized cognitive-behavioral body image therapy with eating disordered women treated in a private clinical practice. *Eating Disorders: The Journal of Treatment and Prevention* 14:31-40.

Olivardia, R. 2002. Body image and muscularity. In *Body Image: A Handbook of Theory, Research, and Clinical Practice*, edited by T. F. Cash and T. Pruzinsky. New York: Guilford Press.

Partridge, J. 2006. *Changing Faces: The Challenge of Facial Disfigurement.* 5th ed. London: Changing Faces.

Pennebaker, J. W. 1997. Writing about emotional experiences as a therapeutic process. *Psychological Science* 8:162-166.

———. 2004. *Writing to Heal: A Guided Journal for Recovering from Trauma and Emotional Upheaval.* Oakland, CA: New Harbinger Publications.

Pennebaker, J. W., and C. K Chung. 2007. Expressive writing, emotional upheavals, and health. In *Foundations of Health Psychology*, edited by H. S. Friedman and R. C. Silver. New York: Oxford University Press.

Phillips, K. A. 2002. Body image and body dysmorphic disorder. In *Body Image: A Handbook of Theory, Research, and Clinical Practice*, edited by T. F. Cash and T. Pruzinsky. New York: Guilford Press.

———. 2005. *The Broken Mirror: Understanding and Treating Body Dysmorphic Disorder.* Rev. ed. New York: Oxford University Press.

Polivy, J., and P. Herman. 1983. *Breaking the Diet Habit.* New York: Basic Books.

———. 1992. Undieting: A program to help people stop dieting. *International Journal of Eating Disorders* 11:261-268.

Pope, H. G., Jr., K. A. Phillips, and R. Olivardia. 2000. *The Adonis Complex: The Secret Crisis of Male Body Obsession.* New York: Free Press.

Powell, M. R., and B. Hendricks. 1999. Body schema, gender, and other correlates in nonclinical populations. *Genetic, Social, and General Psychology Monographs* 125:333-412.

Pruzinsky, T., and M. Edgerton. 1990. Body-image change in cosmetic plastic surgery. In *Body Images: Development, Deviance, and Change*, edited by F. Cash and T. Pruzinsky. New York: Guilford Press.

Ramirez, E. M., and J. C. Rosen. 2001. A comparison of weight control and weight control plus body image therapy for obese men and women. *Journal of Consulting and Clinical Psychology* 69:440-446.

Rieves, L., and T. F. Cash. 1996. Reported social developmental factors associated with women's body-image attitudes. *Journal of Social Behavior and Personality* 11:63-78.

Roberts, A., T. F. Cash, A. Feingold, and B. T. Johnson. 2006. Are black-white differences in females' body dissatisfaction decreasing? A meta-analytic review. *Journal of Consulting and Clinical Psychology* 74:1121-1131.

Rodin, J., L. R. Silberstein, and R. H. Striegel-Moore. 1985. Women and weight: A normative discontent. In *Nebraska Symposium on Motivation: Psychology and Gender,* edited by T. B. Sonderegger. Lincoln: University of Nebraska Press.

Rosen, J. C., P. Orosan, and J. Reiter. 1995. Cognitive behavior therapy for negative body image in obese women. *Behavior Therapy* 26:25-42.

Rosen, J. C., J. Reiter, and P. Orosan. 1995. Cognitive-behavioral body-image therapy for body dysmorphic disorder. *Journal of Consulting and Clinical Psychology* 63:263-269.

Rosen, J. C., E. Saltzberg, and D. Srebnik. 1989. Cognitive behavior therapy for negative body image. *Behavior Therapy* 20:393-404.

Rucker, C. E., and T. F. Cash. 1992. Body images, body-size perceptions, and eating behaviors among African-American and white college women. *International Journal of Eating Disorders* 12:291-300.

Rudiger, J. A., T. F. Cash, M. Roehrig, and J. K. Thompson. 2007. Day-to-day body-image states: Prospective predictors of intra-individual level and variability. *Body Image: An International Journal of Research* 4:1-9.

Rumsey, N. 2002. Body image and congenital conditions with visible differences. In *Body Image: A Handbook of Theory, Research, and Clinical Practice,* edited by T. F. Cash and T. Pruzinsky. New York: Guilford Press.

Rumsey, N., and D. Harcourt. 2004. Body image and disfigurement: Issues and interventions. *Body Image: An International Journal of Research* 1:83-97.

———. 2005. *The Psychology of Appearance.* Berkshire, England: Open University Press.

Sarwer, D. B., T. Pruzinsky, T. F. Cash, R. M. Goldwyn, J. A. Persing, and L. A. Whitaker (eds.). 2006. *Psychological Aspects of Reconstructive and Cosmetic Plastic Surgery: Clinical, Empirical, and Ethical Perspectives.* Philadelphia: Lippincott, Williams & Wilkins.

Sarwer, D. B., J. K. Thompson, and T. F. Cash. 2005. Obesity and body image in adulthood. *Psychiatric Clinics of North America* 28:69-87.

Sarwer, D. B., T. A. Wadden, and G. Foster. 1998. Assessment of body image dissatisfaction in obese women: Specificity, severity and clinical significance. *Journal of Consulting and Clinical Psychology* 66:651-654.

Schwartz, M. B., and K. D. Brownell. 2002. Obesity and body image. In *Body Image: A Handbook of Theory, Research, and Clinical Practice,* edited by T. F. Cash and T. Pruzinsky. New York: Guilford Press.

———. 2004. Obesity and body image. *Body Image: An International Journal of Research* 1:43-56.

Segal, Z. V., J. M. G. Williams, and J. D. Teasdale. 2002. *Mindfulness-Based Cognitive Therapy for Depression: A New Approach to Preventing Relapse.* New York: Guilford Press.

Shontz, F. C. 1990. Body image and physical disability. In *Body Images: Development, Deviance, and Change,* edited by T. F. Cash and T. Pruzinsky. New York: Guilford Press.

Smolak, L. 2002. Body image development in children. In *Body Image: A Handbook of Theory, Research, and Clinical Practice*, edited by T. F. Cash and T. Pruzinsky. New York: Guilford Press.

Stice, E. 2002. Body image and bulimia nervosa. In *Body Image: A Handbook of Theory, Research, and Clinical Practice*, edited by T. F. Cash and T. Pruzinsky. New York: Guilford Press.

————. 2002. Risk and maintenance factors for eating pathology: A meta-analytic review. *Psychological Bulletin* 128:825-848.

Strachan, M. D., and T. F. Cash. 2002. Self-help for a negative body image: A comparison of components of a cognitive-behavioral program. *Behavior Therapy* 33:235-251.

Striegel-Moore, R. H., and D. L. Franko. 2002. Body image issues among girls and women. In *Body Image: A Handbook of Theory, Research, and Clinical Practice*, edited by T. F. Cash and T. Pruzinsky. New York: Guilford Press.

Tantleff-Dunn, S., and J. L. Gokee. 2002. Interpersonal influences on body image development. In *Body Image: A Handbook of Theory, Research, and Clinical Practice*, edited by T. F. Cash and T. Pruzinsky. New York: Guilford Press.

Thompson, J. K. (ed.). 1996. *Body Image, Eating Disorders, and Obesity: An Integrative Guide for Assessment and Treatment*. Washington, DC: American Psychological Association.

————. 2004. *Handbook of Eating Disorders and Obesity*. Hoboken, NJ: Wiley.

Thompson, J. K., and G. Cafri (eds.) 2007. *The Muscular Ideal: Psychological, Social, and Medical Perspectives*. Washington, DC: American Psychological Association.

Thompson, J. K., L. J. Heinberg, M. Altabe, and S. Tantleff-Dunn. 1999. *Exacting Beauty: Theory, Assessment, and Treatment of Body Image Disturbance*. Washington, DC: American Psychological Association.

Thompson, J. K., and L. Smolak (eds.). 2001. *Body Image, Eating Disorders, and Obesity in Youth: Assessment, Prevention, and Treatment*. Washington, DC: American Psychological Association.

Tiggemann, M. 2002. Media influences on body image development. In *Body Image: A Handbook of Theory, Research, and Clinical Practice*, edited by T. F. Cash and T. Pruzinsky. New York: Guilford Press.

————. 2004. Body image across the adult life span: Stability and change. *Body Image: An International Journal of Research* 1:29-41.

Tucker, K. L., D. M. Martz, L. A. Curtin, and B. G. Bazzini. 2007. Examining "fat talk" experimentally in a female dyad: How are women influenced by another woman's body presentation style? *Body Image: An International Journal of Research* 4:157-164.

Veale, D. 2004. Advances in a cognitive behavioural model of body dysmorphic disorder. *Body Image: An International Journal of Research* 1:113-125.

Wertheim, E. H., S. J. Paxton, and S. Blaney. 2004. Risk factors for the development of body image disturbances. In *Handbook of Eating Disorders and Obesity*, edited by J. K. Thompson. Hoboken, NJ: Wiley.

Westmoreland-Corson, P., and A. E. Andersen. 2002. Body image issues among boys and men. In *Body Image: A Handbook of Theory, Research, and Clinical Practice*, edited by T. F. Cash and T. Pruzinsky. New York: Guilford Press.

Whitbourne, S. K., and K. M. Skultety. 2002. Body image development: Adulthood and aging. In *Body Image: A Handbook of Theory, Research, and Clinical Practice*, edited by T. F. Cash and T. Pruzinsky. New York: Guilford Press.

Wiederman, M. W. 2002. Body image and sexual functioning. In *Body Image: A Handbook of Theory, Research, and Clinical Practice*, edited by T. F. Cash and T. Pruzinsky. New York: Guilford Press.

Wilhelm, S. 2006. *Feeling Good about the Way You Look*. New York: Guilford Press.

Williams, E. F., T. F. Cash, and M. T. Santos. 2004. Positive and negative body image: Precursors, correlates, and consequences. Poster presented at the Conference of the Association for Advancement of Behavior Therapy, New Orleans.

Williams, P., and T. F. Cash. 2001. Effects of a circuit weight training program on the body images of college students. *International Journal of Eating Disorders* 30:75-82.

Williamson, D. A., T. M. Stewart, M. A. White, and E. York-Crowe. 2002. An information-processing perspective on body image. In *Body Image: A Handbook of Theory, Research, and Clinical Practice*, edited by T. F. Cash and T. Pruzinsky. New York: Guilford Press.

Winzelberg, A. J., L. Abascal, and C. B. Taylor. 2002. Psychoeducational approaches to the prevention and change of negative body image. In *Body Image: A Handbook of Theory, Research, and Clinical Practice*, edited by T. F. Cash and T. Pruzinsky. New York: Guilford Press.

Yamamiya, Y., T. F. Cash, S. E. Melnyk, H. D. Posavac, and S. S. Posavac. 2005. Women's exposure to thin-and-beautiful media images: Body image effects of media-ideal internalization and impact-education interventions. *Body Image: An International Journal of Research* 2:74-80.

Yamamiya, Y., T. F. Cash, and J. K. Thompson. 2006. Sexual experiences among college women: The differential effects of general versus contextual body images. *Sex Roles* 55:421-427.

Thomas F. Cash, Ph.D., is a true pioneer in the psychology of physical appearance. He is professor emeritus of psychology at Old Dominion University in Norfolk, VA. He is the founding editor-in-chief of *Body Image: An International Journal of Research* and has published six books and more than 200 scholarly articles on topics related to body image and human appearance, including *What Do You See When You Look in the Mirror?* and *The Body Image Handbook.* Dr. Cash's professional website is located at www.body-images.com. He currently resides in Naples, FL.